LOGIC AND ECONOMICS

FREE GROWTH AND OTHER SURPRISES

GORDON GETTY

Logic and Economics: Free Growth and Other Surprises
By Gordon Getty
1. BUS069030 2. BUS029000 3. BUS092000
ISBN: 978-1-935953-96-8
Library of Congress Control Number: 2018947052

Cover design by Lewis Agrell
Author Cover Photo by Gian Andrea Di Stefano

Printed in the United States of America

Authority Publishing
11230 Gold Express Dr. #310-413
Gold River, CA 95670
800-877-1097
www.AuthorityPublishing.com

CONTENTS

FOREWORD BY THE AUTHOR

WHY THIS BOOK?

A year ago, Robert Trivers was kind enough to send me his latest book. The title is *Wild Life*. Perfect two ways. Bob is a world authority on wildlife, to wit evolutionary biology. But his books and papers about that are already well known. This one is about his own wild life, with his ideas in the background. Try it. It's Bob's real voice. One of his papers, co-authored by Huey Newton(!), is about deception and self-deception. I never saw much of either in Bob. I never saw a guy less anxious to impress. Fine if you knew his achievements, and fine if you didn't. What he wanted to talk about was great new ideas by others. It was from him that I first heard about the Hamilton-Zuk parasite theory, where males carrying genes resistant to the current parasite prove it in tournaments or beauty contests, and Paul Ewald's complementary one about parasites stabilizing population density of hosts by evolving more virulent strains when hosts overcrowd. Both are beautiful examples of the obvious-in-hindsight.

I realized that my own book, which I had already started, could take a cue from his. My own life hasn't been wild. It has been interesting because the genius of my father gave me interesting places to be and things to do. I could say something about that.

But the book would be mostly about my ideas in economics. Bob's ideas are well known to anyone in his field. Mine aren't. I'm ten years older than Bob, without much to show for it except in composition. (My last two operas have been getting some traction, and my SACDs get pretty good radio time.) So I'll run my economic ideas up the flagpole, in my real voice, and see if they prove deception or self-deception or something worth the while.

Style Points

Style at its best is artful artlessness. It's as calculated as baiting a hook and reeling in a fish. But it has to be authentic. We know that the fish knows that we know exactly what is going on. We know that the fish is way ahead of us. That's why Bob Trivers and I write what we think in our own voice. Otherwise deception becomes self-deception, the fish goes on to a game worth playing, and we fail in both jobs together.

My brand of artful artlessness can change as my perspectives do. Those shift in little things or big things. For one recent change, I now follow the modern practice preferring "she" when either gender is meant. I swore for years that I would stick to the traditional "he." Down with political correctness! Eventually it seeped through that I had got that backward. I'm an old-fashioned sort who won't sit or eat before a woman does. Replacing "he" with "she," except where the vibes are iffy, is what I should have been doing all along. Feminism was about reversing every gender figure-type. Hurricanes should be male, God female. Why should I object when it was right by accident?

Meanwhile we all learn from the masters. Hemingway knew that short sentences, like short punches, are good for assertion and finality. Henry James knew that long ones fit the nuanced and reflective and tentative. There are some of both moods in all of us. Any composer knows that both are part of the story. But this book favors the first. The mood that comes through is confidence because I'm sold on what I'm selling.

I guess that explains why my sentences will tend toward the simple and short. Short ones fit no-brainers. That doesn't mean I expect a clean score. There will be blunders. I catch a few with every reading. My style is to jump to conclusions, and jump back again when I see what's wrong with them. Sometimes I'm too slow to jump back. Self-deception happens. I'll show how I kept kidding myself about one idea for years. But most of the shockers in this book, including free growth theory and what I call the pay and Y rules and depreciation theory, *are* no-brainers. The logic is unanswerable, or the evidence is, or both are. That's why writing it was fun.

DECLARING MY BIASES

I'm a big free market fan. I would love it even if I agreed with socialists that there is something inherently iniquitous about it. There are bad guys and conflicted motives in markets and government both. What I love about it is the chance to prove ideas. I love Wall Street innovations such as swaps and futures and ETFs (Exchange Traded Funds) and mortgage-backed securities, even admitting their dangers. And who would have thought that the San Francisco Bay area, a stronghold of political correctness at the voters' booth, would nonetheless innovate Siri and Alexa and Tesla and other driverless cars, in its free market havens here and there, over the past five years? Remind me of the last innovation by a committee. It takes individuals, and it takes ones who *prefer* the impossible. It takes guys like my father.

Yes, that was J. Paul Getty. I'll declare a bias for him. His faults were just what we read they were. I liked them fine. My times with him, with an exception I'll note in Chapter 1, are some of my favorite memories. I seem to be the opposite of pharaohs who began their reigns by chiseling off their father's names from the monuments and substituting their own. That was something about a ticket to the afterlife. I put my father's name on things I build. The afterlife will come as it comes.

Since this book is about growth first, I should say how I feel about growth. Most economists, who I'm anything but, treat it as a goal. I love innovation, which has translated to growth, while worrying plenty about growth itself. What happens when anyone can make a doomsday weapon on his desktop? Depressed people do away with themselves every day. Some might take the rest of the world with them if they could. Armageddonist religions wouldn't be needed. Not even destructive intentions need be. A doomsday weapon bought at the five and ten might go off by accident.

Then why do I root for innovation when I'm scared stiff about its consequences? Because alternatives are scarier still. Humans will innovate anyhow, while Big Brother or the religious authorities aren't looking, and I don't like the prospects of innovation driven underground. We'll have to find some way to face the risks and manage them. This book doesn't say how.

On politics, I'm about equally fed up with the killjoy philosophies of homogenization to the left and theocracy to the right. A plague on both their bases! I vote for the candidate that scares me less. This segues into my gut feel about people and the world. Although I'm not an optimist in the sense of making rosy predictions, I am in evaluations. I'm two-thirds Panglossian. (Doctor Pangloss was the guy in Voltaire's *Candide* who said that this is the best of all possible worlds.) I side with the good doctor in that I cannot imagine an improvement to this world or to the human race. I see the dangers and evils as somehow part of the scheme. The world would not be better if it posed no threats and challenges to solve. To solve them is not to wish them away. The stories of Aladdin's lamp and the monkey's paw tell us that each wish after the first is to undo the one before. I think that's what Shaw was telling us in *Don Juan in Hell.* Don Juan and the others are free to go to heaven whenever they like, and occasionally do. They come back because they can't stand the boredom.

Where I find fault, and differ with Pangloss, is as to the doctrines we are taught. Whatever I study, I seem to find a good measure of nonsense taught along with wisdom. This book is about what I find of both in economics. And a problem I try to solve, not wish away, is the danger of losing sight of the points on which Pangloss was right. There is beauty beyond reach in this world, let alone the next, and beauty inside ourselves. The job of verse and music is to remind us.

And I'll admit a bias for the surprises my title promises. I love upending what we had all assumed. Fun! And all the more fun when I can show that famous economists had already seen and said some of the same things I do when we read those economists again. Surprise need not be true novelty. My free growth theory is really John Stuart Mill's, although no one seems to have noticed the paragraph I quote from him. My next-generation theory really belongs to my seventeenth-century rhymesake Sir William Petty, who happens to be my nominee for greatest economist of all time. In a way, I could also credit it to the period of production theorists John Rae, Nassau Senior, William Stanley Jevons and Eugen von Böhm-Bawerk. They reasoned that rates are reciprocals of periods, meaning that either divided into one gives the other, so that the reciprocal of the period of production, if we knew it, would give the rate of production or return. They were right. But they couldn't figure out the period. I'll argue that they need only to have considered human and total capital as explained by Petty two centuries before.

This reveals my bias for economic history. It seems dry as a bone until you find something terrific like those insights. It happens that I had written both theories, and published one, decades before I found those great precedents. Should I have been chagrined? Of course not. Forgotten or unnoticed precedents are at least as much fun to point out as the surprises they showed ahead of me.

I will also reveal a bias for evolutionary biology. Its main axiom, the biological imperative, becomes one of mine. The idea is that behaviors are selected for successful reproduction. I will try to show that the classical school treated this as axiomatic from Petty through his famous successors Adam Smith, Francois Quesnay, Thomas Malthus, David Ricardo, Senior and Mill. Malthus was only the most obvious case. It lapsed from attention when a brilliant new insight called marginalism preferred to do without explanations for tastes. That indifference lasted for about a century. Biology has now made its way back into economics, partly because the selfish-gene idea seemed to fit the model of Adam Smith's "invisible hand" weaving cooperation out of practical self-interest. I will try to put this another way.

Above all comes my bias for the great thinkers in those fields. We saw that as to Bob Trivers. Although I often cite them to disagree with them, I see all as giants from whose shoulders I slip in trying to climb. I don't kick sand on 98-pound weaklings. Mill was a *mensch* who gives us all lessons in attribution and generosity, particularly to schools he disputed, and who nonetheless didn't mind being a minority of one in his books or in parliament.

Petty was something beyond. Polymath, self-made tycoon, anatomist, music teacher, father of national accounts, originator of present value theory and human capital and next generation theory, and esteemed by both Smith and Karl Marx for other innovations I don't mention. Such men are understood slowly and incompletely.

WHY SCIENCE AND ART?

The business of science is to take man off his high horse, and to measure him and the horse by the same evolutionary ruler. The business of comedy is about the same. Somewhere Arthur Miller said "tragedy is uplift, and comedy takes us back to earth again." He was right. The horse bucks, and we're down from our lofty perch to our backsides. We laugh because the view from there is the same beauty from the other direction.

Art at its best brings us back up. If I were the lawyer for mankind on Judgment Day, I would remind the Court of *Hamlet, Tristan und Isolde* and the Gettysburg address. The view from there is of something that holds, even when the world falls and the dead rise on Judgment Day. Only people, may it please the Court, have conceived such things. The horse and the horselaugh reverse the perspective, and will forever, and must. Our fallibility and pratfallability are part of the beauty that holds.

OUTLINE OF THE ARGUMENTS

The plural in this heading is unusual. Shouldn't a book follow a single overriding argument? This one does in a way. What pulls the arguments together is a prioritization of logic and philosophy. While science tends to predict the rule from the data, philosophy tends to reverse the direction. The bottom-up scientific method doesn't get far in economics because market data reveal little about human capital, which is some two-thirds to four-fifths of all capital in most judgments, including mine, beyond its rental cost in pay. The best economics can do is feel its way in the dark from assumption to prediction, as a rule, and then look for ways to scrape together enough market data for a test.

What I came up with, listed alphabetically, includes:

- **Bank Devolution:** Commercial banks accept deposits and make loans. They fail periodically, or need help, because they can't attract investors without dangerous deposit/investment leverage. They should and probably will devolve into deposit banks that invest deposits in ETFs (Exchange Traded Funds) and other mutual funds, along with unaffiliated lending banks that raise money from investors. Shock value: deposit-and-lend banks have been central to economies for eight centuries. I say stop now.

- **Depreciation Theory:** Depreciation begins near zero and then rises to become substantially all of cash flow as human or asset life ends. I'll say no more of the argument now but that it is exactly as with mortgage amortization. Shock value: business and economic tradition, trusting adversely selective evidence, teach the opposite.

- **Free Growth Theory:** Investment beyond depreciation plowback, at the scale of all investors together, adds nothing to capital value. Growth happens when capital evolves more productive forms at no additional cost. Logic: the market bets on the future, and capitalizes promising ideas without waiting for products to appear and red ink to turn into black. Proof: charts and tables showing that the ratio of consumption to capital holds constant in capital accelerations. Shock value: tax law is formed on the assumption that faster growth costs consumption deferment first.

- **Inflation-Protected Dollars (DIPS):** Real (disinflated) dollars can and should become legal tender right now. Cell phone apps can track the inflation index chosen and do the math at point of sale, as in paying in Euros versus pounds in London. I'll go into the mechanics. Shock value: none except that we all missed something so obvious.

- **Market Money:** Some securities, particularly ETFs, combine competitive return with instant liquidity. They make up a money supply which brings no inflation risk as it rises, since its owners can hold it indefinitely for return while left unspent. Shock value: monetary theory has not accounted for this exception.

- **Next Generation Theory:** Petty conjectured that the period over which investment is meant to be recovered is the age difference between generations. His reason seems to have been the biological imperative; our top priority is to get the next generation into place. I'll show why I agree. I use R.A. Fisher's method to model the generation gap ("generation length") here today at 28.5 years. I interpret this as the period of production Rae and others would look for two centuries later, but before allowance for capital growth. Its reciprocal comes to 3.5% per year. I model this as the average-risk cash flow rate, or rate of return less capital growth rate. Shock value: many today accept an old tradition that return converges to the output growth rate, and to zero in growthlessness (the "stationary state"). Evidence over three millennia supports my argument, adapted from Petty's, that return in the stationary state runs about 3.5% per year. Add growth, and return becomes about 3.5% plus whatever the current capital growth rate happens to be.

- **Depreciation Recovery Rule:** Human depreciation has been part of the daily vocabulary of human capital economists since work by Nobelist Theodore Schultz and others in the early 1960s. It is the steady drain in present value of our remaining lifetime cash flow (essentially pay once we reach adulthood) as time leaves fewer paydays still to come. Yet I find no statement by Schultz or anyone as to where this huge flow goes. Drain to where? A famous study by Yoram Ben-Porath in 1967 treats it implicitly as deadweight loss. My impression is that others have seen it that way too, but I cannot find an explicit statement one way or the other. I argue that it must be recovered in product value and revenue (pay) for the same reason as with plant depreciation; we would not have invested otherwise. The shock value is in this inference for pay, which is taught to compensate the worker's current output alone rather than that plus human depreciation.

- **Risk Theory:** Each individual acquires or adapts assets to suit her current degree of risk/return tolerance. This is equally true of human capital, which cannot be traded but is particularly adaptable through behavior modification. One interesting inference is that human capital, which is owned disproportionately by the risk-prone young, figures to be the factor higher in risk/return. Another is that the business sector, which tends to find more or less the same owners as the housing sector, should not differ much from it in risk and return. Shock value: even after the subprime crisis, many hold to the old faith that houses are safer.

- **Output Rule:** Basic teachings in finance and human capital economics combine to show that output (creation of value) equals consumption plus investment (growth in capital excluding human capital) plus self-invested work (defined by Schultz) less human depreciation. Shock value: all macroeconomics and national accounts are founded on the doctrine that output equals consumption plus investment, pure and simple.

- **Pay Rule:** The recovery rule, together with Schultz' distinction between self-invested and realized (marketed) work, suggests that pay is expected to compensate realized work plus human depreciation. I will cover other possibilities, one proposed by Adam Smith's friend Quesnay, and show why I rule them out. Shock value: none once we accept the real shocker in the recovery rule.

ACKNOWLEDGMENTS

Examples just listed make it clear that this book is too subversive to blame on any but myself. With that blanket exoneration, I would like to thank Claire Brown, Mike Cagney, David Darst, Mike Dooley, Bob Frank, Oliver Goodenough, Brian Mannix, Jeff Londale, Kevin McCabe, Jean Paul Rabanal, Paul Romer, Evan Smith, Bob Trivers and Paul Zak for their valiant efforts to make me see the light. I thank the ghosts of all past economists listed in these pages, and apologize to them for any damage from the grappling hooks with which I have tried to scramble to their shoulders. I thank Piketty and Zucman, on behalf of the world, for their immense gift of their website. I thank Mac for my computer and Microsoft for its Excel software, although both are commercial products rather than gifts, because I couldn't demonstrate free growth without those as well as the website. Finally, I thank any reader who has made it even this far through my quirky dissections of the esoteric.

1

SO WHO AM I TO TALK?

I never finished a course in economics. I started one at the University of San Francisco sixty years ago, and dropped it when I couldn't see the foundations. But the bug had bitten me. I knew that one day I would try on my own.

I always loved logic. My favorite philosophers at USF were the pre-Socratics who liked nothing better than to confound common sense. One example was Zeno the Eleatic and his argument that Achilles can never catch up to the tortoise; Achilles must first reach the line where the tortoise was last, and the tortoise has since moved on. Logic can play such tricks. But I sensed that economics was the place to try its limits. Dropping the course didn't mean giving up, and logic would be the key.

Neither did I take a course in business administration or investment. My major was English literature. As a grade schooler I had asked my father about this. Where and what should I end up studying? He had read economics and petro-leum geology at Oxford, and I supposed he would advise something like that for me. I got a surprise. Career-oriented majors were fine but not necessary. A grounding in the liberal arts could be as much or more. The trick was to learn how to learn. That sounded right, and anyhow right for me. So I chose USF, a twenty-minute walk from home until my mother moved us to San Rafael, a half-hour drive across the Golden Gate Bridge, and followed my intuitions toward English lit and history and music and philosophy.

I graduated with a degree in English lit in 1956. This was the time of skittish peace between the Korean and Vietnam wars, and the Reserve Forces Act meant I had to report for six months active duty starting in the spring of '57. Meanwhile I worked for my father. I and my brother Paul, later Sir Paul, started at the bottom pumping gas and changing oil at separate gas stations not far from our home in San Rafael. That left time for a few weeks at a bulk plant (oil warehouse and tank farm) in San Francisco, still working at the bottom, before I reported. Paul had served in the Korean War, and was now exempt. I was a shavetail second lieutenant, thanks to the ROTC program at USF, in the quartermaster branch at Fort Lee, Virginia. My eyesight was never good enough for the combat branches.

Ike, who was then president, had started in the quarter-master too. My military career was not so glorious. Somehow I finished the six months at Fort Lee and seven and half years of inactive duty following, obligating me to one week-end per month at military posts near home, without being

2

promoted even to first lieutenant. By policy, I should have been promoted or busted to the ranks. My attendance had been spotty, and I should probably have been busted. I later learned that my school chum Manuel Teles, who worked at Fort Presidio in San Francisco, had somehow fixed the record. Thank God for old friends.

My weekends of saluting were postponed when Paul and I went back to work for my father in 1958. My father then lived in the Ritz Hotel in Paris. He liked ordinary two-room suites. The sitting room was his office. His filing system was a steamer trunk. Our job was to sit and listen as he met with executives or art people or old friends. He would usually take us along to lunch and dinner, and wangle us in when he had been invited somewhere. He was the world's most attentive father whenever we were with him, at least, if focused on other things when we weren't.

Paul went on to learn refining and marketing in Italy, after those few weeks in Paris, while I went to the oilfields my father had just found and developed in the Neutral Zone between Saudi Arabia and Kuwait. Paul soon learned Italian, became general manager within two years, and ran things well. I learned only a little Arabic, but also became manager in 1959, and soon blundered my way into two weeks' house arrest. I had got crossways with the local emir, Mohammed bin Nasr, not a bad guy, about perks and privileges he and his staff expected Getty Oil to pay for.

The case against me was rigged. One of our junior staff drivers, a Kuwaiti I think, had accidentally rammed and damaged a pipeline. He had fled the country to avoid jail.

Jails there were no fun. His supervisor, Jim Kinnell, was warned that he (Jim) was accountable under Saudi law, and would be sent to jail instead. Jim came to me. I realized what was brewing. Laws are flexible, and Jim would have got off with a caution at most if I weren't at odds with the Emir. I was obviously next. But I was not about to gamble that the threat to Jim was a bluff. I told him that if I were in his shoes, I would go back to England. He did. That left me. But I was in my shoes. The blunders had been mine, and I would face the music.

My two weeks of house arrest went peacefully. The plain cement-blocks had been built for my father at our port camp of Mina Saud when he lived in the Neutral Zone in 1953. The Emir's identical house was a few steps away. My father's favorite maple sugar was still in the fridge. I read the few Shakespeare plays I hadn't read in college, and read or reread the complete poems and plays of John Keats.

The house arrest was probably as much dressing-down as I deserved. Paul, or anyone else, would have handled the perks and privileges more adroitly. But our host country, Saudi Arabia, may have picked up on something too. Getty Oil was not one of the concession companies in the Middle East named in the baksheesh (bribery) scandals that made the front pages over the few years remaining before most concessions were negotiated away and host countries ran things themselves.

Back to my father in Scotland, where he was visiting his old friends the Maxwells near Inverness, and then to the two-room suite at the Ritz in London about like the one in Paris. He drove the six hundred miles between, in a vintage Cadillac, taking two days and stopping to visit historic sites and museums. He needed no guidebook. I sat in on meetings and events everywhere with him in London as in Paris. I assumed that the Saudis had cleared the house arrest with him, and I would have agreed as he did. He too was in different shoes. He was right. He had solved a real problem with minimum damage. Lesson learned, and no hard feelings either way.

It was clear to both of us that I was not cut out to be a line officer, meaning one who runs things from day to day. My mind goes off on tangents instead of tracking arguments in real time. That works for me, but not as an administrator. We decided to try me as a consultant.

That began at my father's Spartan Aircraft Company in Tulsa, Oklahoma. He hadn't meant to buy it. He had bought control of Skelly Oil, centered in Tulsa, and Spartan turned out to be one of its holdings. Then came Pearl Harbor. My father was 48 years old, and had been a yachtsman. He took a navigation course at USC along with kids half his age, led the class, and volunteered for sea duty. His old friend James Forrestal, Secretary of the Navy, steered him to Spartan instead. Spartan could make training planes and could train pilots. My father accepted. He paid himself a salary of one dollar a year.

He had decisions to make when MacArthur and Shigemitsu signed the peace treaty. Training planes were not meant to leave the ground. Spartan lacked the capacity to make the real thing up to competition. The demand for training planes pretty much ended with the war. My father could sell out or find another use. He decided to make house trailers. It worked. I had lived in a Spartan trailer in the Neutral Zone, like the rest of the senior staff, when I stayed at our Wafra oil field rather than the house at Mina Saud. We and the market had liked them fine.

Herschel Shelton had been one of my father's right-hand men during the conversion to trailers. He said that the place to look for him was never in his office. You would find him in overalls under a trailer on the factory floor, with a welding iron or riveting gun. He liked to be able to do any job his workers did. How else would he know if they were doing it right?

I stayed in my father's house at Spartan, as at Mina Saud. It stood at the opposite end of the landing field from the offices and trailer plant. I drove another seasoned Cadillac that my father had left in case he came back. Max Balfour, who ran Spartan, called it a clunker. It clunked me around the countryside on weekends, or to Jamil's restaurant or Cap Balfour's house for dinner, or downtown to the movies or symphony or opera house. Cap (Captain) Balfour had flown in World War I, and showed crippled hands from when his plane caught fire. He was cranky, urbane and razor-sharp. His problem was that Spartan couldn't seem to come out in the black. He worshipped my father, and figured he had let him down. He seems to have brought his moods with him after work, which my father generally didn't. That cost him his sunny young wife. I somehow got a pass. I could understand him, and I was my father's son.

My advice in the end was that my father should sell. Meanwhile I was taking an interest in economics again. Business was about rate of return. Spartan's was negative. What was the benchmark? I did a little study.

It is easy to see that return tends to even out from one company or industry to the next. We pour investment into high-return prospects, and unintentionally drive that high return down toward the norm by expanding the capital denominator. I didn't know that Robert Turgot had written the same in 1766. But what struck me was the impression that return, net of inflation, seemed to revert to a norm over time. Why were interest rates, averaged over business cycles, about the same then as in Dante's time or Julius Caesar's? Why should human impatience be a steady norm? That puzzle nagged me for about a quarter century until I found the answer. Another decade or two would pass before I learned that Sir William Petty had found it in the seventeenth century.

I went home in 1961 to study harmony and counterpoint at the San Francisco Conservatory of Music. I had found time to compose a few things at the house at Mina Saud with a piano I had bought in Kuwait. They included an *a cappella* (unaccompanied) choral setting of Tennyson's "All Along the Valley," and something to which I later fit Emily Dickinson's poem "Beauty Crowds Me" in my song cycle "The White Election." The composer Charles Haubiel published "All Along the Valley" in his Composers' Press in Los Angeles in 1959. The one change he suggested, an unexpected D flat major resolution, is the best touch in the piece. I had noticed copies in music shops in Tulsa. So it seemed about time to develop that interest too, and the conservatory back home seemed the logical place.

I studied there from fall 1961 through spring 1962. I was probably the only composition student already published. My teacher in both the fall and spring classes was Sol Joseph. He was a legend there. Most of what he taught confirmed my instincts. Maybe five percent was old rules I didn't think much of, and five percent good ideas that hadn't occurred to me. All was useful anyhow as a guide to what leading authorities have thought and taught. That was the point. We were to accept what we liked, and anyhow learn the lingo.

Those two courses covered traditions of the eighteenth and nineteenth centuries. Most composers in the 1960s, and probably some or most of my classmates, thought of that as a stepping stone toward study of the serialism and other atonalism then in vogue. I skipped those classes. I realized that I was a nineteenth-century composer at heart. Now the world seems to have spun back to where I was all along. For most composers now, atonalism is one of the colors on our palettes. Even I use some. So did Bach. We reach for that color when we want to express disorientation or angst. I found I could get more said most of the time with major-minor scales.

Five short piano pieces I wrote then were published by Belwin Mills in 1964. As my father's son, you might imagine that I was asked to pay the costs. Nope. Neither had I paid a cent to Composers' Press. Vanity press exists, but that was not the business model of those two firms. I got standard royalties from sales, not amounting to much, and they got the rest.

Six published pieces by age 31 would not have impressed Mozart or Schubert. By lesser standards, it was a pretty good start. There are distinguished composers who have never found a publisher. Tomorrow the world! I would write operas and symphonies! What happened instead was sixteen years of writer's block, or eighteen since finishing the pieces in 1962. I suppose I was trying to say "Shazam!" and turn into something I wasn't. The ice would break in 1980, when I realized that Billy Batson would have to do. But that gets me ahead of my story.

I married Ann in 1964, making it a banner year on that count even more than the publication, and went back to work for my father. That took us to New York in 1965. Tidewater Oil Company, which would merge into its parent Getty Oil Company a few years later, had red ink problems in its Eastern Division. My job was to see why. Eastern Division was run by "Jim" Jiminez, an upbeat guy I liked. I don't think he took the red-ink problems home with him as Cap Balfour had. He reported to my half-brother George at corporate headquarters in Los Angeles, and George reported to my father in London. George, like Paul, had earned his job by outstanding performance at every level on the way up, which is more than you could say for me in the Neutral Zone. But George was touchy. He had a chip on his shoulder. I think my father liked to ride him, and he sometimes felt unappreciated. You have to shrug that off. George was doing fine. The problem in Eastern Division was not in him, and it was not in Jim Jiminez. Then what?

I looked at the books. The red ink had nothing to do with management. Eastern Division did refining and marketing. Its new refinery in Delaware had been optimized to process heavy Wafra crude oil, which then was over a dollar cheaper per barrel than the lighter and easier-to-refine crude we produced in Texas and the Central Basin. As soon as the new refinery was finished, Washington restricted imports to protect domestic producers. We had to buy pricier crude after all. Tidewater's Western Division refinery at Martinez, by contrast, had all the cheap oil it needed in our own Kern River field. The Martinez refinery was old, and more expensive to operate. But the net advantage still went to Western Division by about a dollar per barrel. Meanwhile gasoline sold for about a dollar less per barrel, although only two or three cents less per gallon, in the refinery-loaded east than in California. That raised the advantage to two dollars.

Management can't do much about import quotas and market conditions. I reported to my father that Eastern Division was at least as well run as Western Division, where the ink was black thanks to cheaper crude and pricier gasoline.

Then could we cut costs or boost receipts in other ways? I proposed that we close our old and inefficient Boston Harbor terminal, where barges unloaded gasoline into our tank farms to be trucked to service stations, and supply Boston from our new terminal at Providence two hours' drive away. If that worked, other distribution consolidations seemed possible. I later proposed much the same thing for our operations in Japan, where the new terminal at Kawasaki could theoretically obviate the older and clumsier one in Tokyo Harbor. I realized that plant-closing might be unthinkable in Japan, but thought that something good might come of the idea.

Sometime a little later came my lawsuit against my father. It isn't my happiest memory. There had been a stock dividend years before, when I was still in school. We had treated it a certain way on the books. I read the law as saying it should have been treated another way. The law was probably on my side, and common sense on my father's. Judge Peery wisely found a way to make common sense win in the end. Meanwhile I had accused my father of nothing worse than oversight. My visits to Sutton Place, now with Ann and the boys, went the same as before. The lawsuit seldom came up and was discussed in easy terms when it did. I suggested to him, for example, that he might want to settle with my stepmother Teddy in case there could be claims by the estate of my late half-brother Timmy. He did. Somehow we got through the lawsuit without bad blood. One would not have guessed that so much was at stake. The stock dividend had been a huge one. What I learned from my father, then most of all, was perspective. He believed in an even keel. Zeno the Stoic, not the Eleatic, would have met his match.

The lawsuit lasted from 1966 through 1971. In hindsight, thank gosh he won. If I had, tax consequences would have been ugly all around. Again I had learned a lesson, and again there were no hard feelings either way.

I continued to do consulting jobs for him throughout the lawsuit and after. I charged expenses, but no fee. And I didn't pad expenses. If I had, you can believe he would have seen it. I stayed in a single room in the best hotels, ate three squares a day, and paid for anything else myself. I was trying to make the point that I didn't want to be paid. Neither had my father at Spartan during the war. The idea was for me to be of use. I was paid like everyone else when working for my father full-time, but never on consulting jobs.

Those now came once or twice a year, and lasted for a week or two each. Composing was still on the back burner. I was keen on physics, economics, human origins and city planning. It became clear that all but the third needed better math skills than I had. So I bought the Barnes and Noble textbook on College Mathematics, got through it in a week of hard work, and then began on the Johnson and Kiokemeister textbook on calculus, along with Halliday and Resnick on physics. Together they took me nearly a year. At the end, I was allowed to sit in on the freshman physics finals at Cal Berkeley, where the same two textbooks were taught.

It was the finals for physics majors, and meant to be tough. Cal took physics seriously. Not every freshman was destined to go farther. Some should be steered towards engineering, which pays better anyhow. There were ten questions. Three hours were allowed. Each of us had a calculator and nothing else. Not even a table of integrals. My

God! I had to remember them or rederive them. There are some that had taken even Newton and Leibnitz months to solve. I don't remember any of the questions. There were 200 to 300 kids in the room. Maybe 20 or 30 Asians, about three women, no blacks. Not one finished early. And some figure to be Nobelists by now. We're talking about *Cal.* I had answered seven questions when the three hours were up. Was that good enough? I got a call in a few days. I passed, and beat the class average.

My old friend Matt Kelly warned me about this time that George was in trouble. Matt had known George's new wife Jackie, and had been invited to dinner there. Matt's impression was of out-of-control mood changes. He said that George at one point had drawn him aside, shown a pistol and warned him about paying too much attention to Jackie. The next minute they were back at the table in jolly spirits. I learned later what was wrong. George thought he had a weight problem, although I never noticed one. Doctors prescribed amphetamines in those days to control appetite. They revved him up and made it hard to sleep at night. So the same doctors prescribed barbiturates at night to get him to sleep. Uppers and downers are dangerous enough. Add a drink or two and you've got trouble.

Of course I should have told my father. But I didn't want to be the one. I liked to boost my brothers. Many must have seen the symptoms Matt saw. Let them break the news. But the others must have felt as I did. We waited too long. I got a phone call in 1973. George had died at Mount Sinai Hospital. There was an empty bottle of sleeping pills.

My father's death came in 1976. Ann and I had got word it was coming a few weeks before. We were there. So was Norris Bramblett, an accountant who had worked for my father since I was in school. My father trusted him. So did I. He had only a fourth-grade education, but a PhD's worth of character and sense. My father, Zeno the Stoic when things got tough, cracked jokes to the end. Norris alone could understand him by then. He translated patiently. My father was giving me one more lesson. He lapsed into a coma. Ann and I were called down from our bedroom when he died.

That left me and Lansing Hays as co-trustees of the trust controlling his companies. Lansing ran the law firm that handled nearly all my father's business and little else. It was a big job. Lansing was smart, abrasive, and dead honest. He didn't mind hurting people's feelings. I was not immune. It didn't matter. It wouldn't have mattered to my father. What mattered was that Lansing knew what trust meant, and put the Trust first. That's what I cared about.

Lansing was already on the Getty Oil board. I was invited to join too. We met four times a year, most often in Los Angeles. Harold Berg, an oil engineer from Colorado, had become CEO and chairman after George died. Sid Petersen, an accountant, was COO. Harold was a warmer and more approachable personality. That's what you'd expect in an oilfield guy. Sid was reserved and analytical. That's what you might expect from an accountant, although Norris Bramblett fit anything but the stereotype. Harold and Sid were both clearly well chosen. Neither then nor later did I doubt that Getty was run at least as well as its big oil rivals.

The board too were top people. But trouble was brewing. The Trust, meaning Lansing and I, owned about 40% of the shares. The Getty Museum, also chaired by Harold, owned another 12%. Boards and managers prefer scattered ownership, so that they can operate more freely. Second-best would be concentration in docile hands happy to follow the board's guidance. But my father had made it clear to Lansing and me that we were to trust our judgment. We should be ready "to vote the management in and out." Since stockholders elect boards and boards hire managers, that meant to vote the board in and out.

No wonder they were concerned. Lansing and I were both boat-rockers. Wouldn't it be safer if there were a corporate co-trustee? These are usually safety-minded banks, and many banks did business with Getty Oil.

Lansing died in 1972. That left me as the sole trustee. I was less obstreperous than Lansing, but also less predictable. Hostile takeovers were common then, where bids are made directly to shareholders rather than cleared through the board. Getty was rich in oil reserves per dollar of share price. It could be a target. Board members tend to feel that they know stockholders' interests best, and that the angels are on the side of "friendly" or board-approved takeovers if any at all. Stockholders don't necessarily feel that way.

Temperatures rose when I pushed serious study of the possibility of taking Getty private. The idea was to give up our corporate structure to escape the corporate double tax. Management and its investment banker, Goldman Sachs, advised against. I now think they were right, although my idea had good precedents. I pressed on, unwisely, by trying to convince the Museum to back me. They had better sense.

It was time to heal the breach. Marty Lipton of Wachtell, Lipton, a top mergers and acquisitions law firm, represented the Museum. He proposed a moratorium (the "tripartite agreement") where the Trust, Museum and company would hold the status quo for one year. Harold Berg had retired as chairman of Getty Oil, and Sid was now chairman and CEO. His COO was Bob Miller, a keen petroleum engineer. Harold Berg still chaired the Museum, although Harold Williams was its CEO and main voice. We all signed. But Getty Oil had its fingers crossed. A few days later, the company petitioned the court to appoint a co-trustee. It proposed Bank of America. B of A's chairman, Chauncey Medberry, sat on the Getty Oil board. Paul and George's daughters joined the plaintiffs.

The Museum was more outraged than I was. Marty felt that he had been used. He and Harold Williams, a business-savvy guy who had chaired the SEC under Jimmy Carter, realized that if I could be hog-tied, the Museum with its 12% was the next hog.

This was in November of 1983. Within a few weeks, the Museum and I signed a "consent of shareholders" taking over the company. The required public disclosure of this, on top of the tripartite agreement and co-trustee lawsuit before, was blood in the water.

Pennzoil launched a hostile takeover bid in December. My concern was that the trust should not be locked in a minority position. I met with Pennzoil in New York. We resolved that to my satisfaction. The Getty Oil board met, also in New York, on January fourth. The mood was not sunny. Harold Stuart, one of the brightest and finest board members, assumed that I had invited the Pennzoil bid. Chauncey Medberry thought I should be sued. But Sid and the board acted responsibly overall. We countered with a higher price, Pennzoil accepted, and we went home thinking we had a deal.

Texaco offered a higher bid two days later. Was Getty Oil already bound to Pennzoil? Its lawyers and mine said it wasn't until the final agreement was signed. I had my doubts. But I liked Texaco's offer better, and my duty was clear. The Trust and Museum would be paid cash for their shares, rather than locked in. I had insisted on language in the Pennzoil agreement that bound me only as "subject only to my fiduciary obligations." My obligation, in the light of legal advice, was to accept Texaco's offer. I did, and voted the same way as a member of Getty's and the Museum's board. Those were fiduciary obligations too.

Pennzoil sued Texaco, and eventually won damages of some eleven billion dollars. The Museum and Trust had cashed out. We were not parties. The Pennzoil and Texaco filings both spoke well of me. But there was still the lawsuit seeking a corporate co-trustee. That would have been very dangerous before the sale to Texaco cashed us out. A corporate co-trustee might well have assented to "corporate defenses" blocking a sale and effectively locking the trust in a minority position. But now that danger was over. The remaining plaintiffs were my three nieces and Paul. I couldn't blame them. How could a corporate co-trustee hurt?

But I was still worried. I now wanted to split up the trust into four separate ones for my family, Paul's, George's, and my other half-brother Ronnie's. Corporate co-trustees tend to prefer the safety of acting only as required, and anyhow might not be keen to vote themselves out of a job.

Were Paul and my nieces mad at me? Believe it. Lawsuits get that way. Lawyers on both sides say nasty things. That lasted because splitting the Trust took time. The math was easy, but the legal precedents were vague. My lawyer, Mose Lasky, thought we needed new California law. Plaintiffs' counsel didn't think so. I was accused of stalling. Someone had the bright idea to approach Willie Brown as Speaker of the Senate. The law Mose wanted had already worked in other states, and Willie liked it. He pushed it through. Problem solved. The Trust was split into four in 1988, and an unhappy chapter ended. My nieces and I are as close as ever. So were Paul and I until his death in 2002.

My interests by the time of the split were still composing, verse, economics, human origins and evolutionary biology. Composing was going pretty well. My writer's block had melted away eight years before in the summer of 1980. Ann and I and the boys were traveling in Paris then. We wandered into Smith's English language bookstore. I bought the Thomas Johnson variorum of Emily Dickinson's 1800-odd poems. "Variorum" means including Emily's own variations when she mailed the same poem to different people, or put a copy in the chest at the foot of her bed.

I read them all over the next two days. Emily had been one of my favorites at USF. She died in 1886. She had published only eleven poems. Squabbles among the heirs delayed publication of about half the rest until Johnson published them in 1959, three years after I graduated. Many already published had been "bowdlerized" to fit conventional rhyme and grammar. Johnson gave us the real McCoy from her manuscripts. All was new to me.

I had no piano in our hotel room in Paris, but set a few of the poems in my head to write down later. More followed. One of her poems I didn't set begins "Mine by the right of the white election ..." Election meant choice. Her white smock hangs today by her bed in Amherst where she was born and died. White is the color of weddings and burials. Her choice, I think, was a death marriage to the reverend Charles Wadsworth of the Arch Street Church in Philadelphia. He was happily married. She met him about three times in her life. I would tell her story in 31 of her poems, one in two different settings, in my cycle "The White Election."

It was completed in 1981, and broadcast on National Public Radio two years later. It seems to have made a good impression. Slava Rostropovich had kind words, and invited me to write something for cello and orchestra that he could schedule on his upcoming tour in Russia. Placido Domingo invited me to write a song for him. Renata Scotto wanted me to choose five or so of the White Election songs that she could include in her concerts. All were big opportunities. Somehow none happened. Other stuff was coming out the pipeline.

That included my opera *Plump Jack*. Here I would tell the rise and fall of Falstaff in Shakespeare's *Henry IV* and

Henry V. This was riskier. Now the accompaniment would be orchestra, not piano, and I had no background in orchestration. Composing and orchestrating are not the same. Composing is like writing a play, and orchestration is like casting the play. There are composers that don't orchestrate, and orchestrators who don't compose. Most of us do both. I always did my own orchestration because no one else would know what I wanted. I gradually learned from my mistakes. Now I can probably hold my own in orchestration, although many do that better.

Plump Jack was completed scene by scene over some twenty years. I would think it was finished, and then decide it wasn't. My next two operas, each running about an hour, would be composed much faster. I set *Usher House* to my earlier libretto based on Poe's story in about six weeks in 2008 and 2009. *The Canterville Ghost*, on Wilde's short story, took me about two weeks each, with two months between, for libretto, composition and orchestration. The last two operas have been premiered at major opera houses. Usher House ran again at San Francisco Opera. The "scare pair," meaning *Usher* and *Canterville* as a double bill, has now been performed by the Center for Contemporary Opera in New York, and by Los Angeles Opera in June 2018. *Plump Jack* is still waiting its turn.

My interest in human origins led me to the Leakey Foundation. I had read about Louis Leakey in the papers, and had met him a few times in Los Angeles and San Francisco. Brilliant, courtly, fierce. He let you know what was wrong.

I became a fellow in 1973, a trustee the next year and chairman the next.

Clark Howell, who taught anthropology at Berkeley, chaired our science committee. His co-chair was Dave Hamburg, a Stanford psychology professor who specialized in great ape studies or primatology. Most leading scientists in either field were members or regular advisors. They recommended grants, and we trustees funded them. We took a venture capital role, usually making grants of a few thousand dollars to promising new prospects rather than bigger amounts to steady-state projects already proved. Those proved ones included Jane Goodall's chimp studies at Gombe or Richard Leakey's digs at Lake Turkana. National Geographic, or the Wenner Gren or World Wildlife or National Science Foundations tended to fund the known winners. We're a lot bigger now. I am one of the few living links to those great people and times. We've evolved with the science. But we stick to the venture capital role.

That always left time to organize lectures and symposia. A few of us including Nancy Pelosi, long before she tried politics, put together an all-star two-day symposium at the Palace of Fine Arts in the San Francisco Marina district in 1973. Tickets sold out, and hundreds watched on screens set up in the lobby. Julian Huxley regretted, but sent his good wishes on tape. The octogenarian Raymond Dart recounted his discovery of *australopithecus africanus* at Taung cave near Johannesburg in 1924.

Louis Leakey had died the year before, but his equally legendary widow Mary updated us on the digs at Olduvai.

Dick Hay filled us in on the geology there. Jane Goodall gave the news from Gombe. Dave Hamburg reported on the new chimpanzee compound near the linear reactor at Stanford. Clark Howell briefed us on his work at Torralba and Ambrona in Spain, where our ancestors half our size had hunted elephants twice the size of modern ones. (Elephants go back at least as far as their mammoth and mastodon cousins.) Desmond Clark covered African archaeology in general and his discoveries at Kalambo Falls in particular. Sherry Washburn showed the way in which our DNA is 98% the same as a chimp's. All were my close friends.

It was at a symposium in 1974, in Washington I believe, that I first heard and met Irv DeVore. His talk was on evolutionary biology and Hamilton's rule. Both were new to me. Irv was a champion speaker. Students packed his anthropology classes at Harvard. He became a Leakey stalwart and a particularly close friend.

I liked his topic. Genes encode traits, and traits more adaptive to niche pressures are likelier to carry the genes that encode them into the next generation. The likeliness is "fitness." A beauty of this is that you can predict traits from the environment (niche), and the environment from traits. That promised the kind of logical challenge that I loved.

Survival of the fittest was not news to us. What was news was that bright scientists like Irv were specializing in that logic, and making testable predictions for creatures generally, humans included, rather than sticking to the groups they studied most. That meant people I could talk to.

A favorite theme was and is something called Hamilton's rule. The idea is that genes maximize their survival chances by encoding traits to invest fitness in the close kin likeliest to bear copies. Creatures would invest on the condition $rB>C$, where benefit B was fitness gained by the donee or investee, cost C was fitness surrendered by the donor, and r was relatedness between. This fit logic and experience to a point. It troubled me, even so, on grounds I couldn't quite pin down until very recently (May 2017). My adaptation of his rule will show in my version of how biology and economics come together.

Economics was always somewhere on my screen. It was the biggest challenge because I had to reinvent it from scratch. I had dropped the course at USF because I couldn't find the foundations. But we don't build a foundation without knowing what we want to top. I had to reinvent everything at once. Does that mean I thought I was best qualified for such a task? No. Plenty of people are better at logic than I am. Rather I seemed to be the only volunteer.

Explicit economic axioms are seen as a nineteenth-century thing. There are implicit ones to a degree. Macroeconomics is said to rest on microeconomics, called "macro" (big) and "micro" (small) for short. Macro tries to reconcile full employment with stable prices at national scales. Micro tracks the interplay of supply, demand and price at any scale where markets form. Good so far. But I felt the need of a logical context for both. Too darned much was being taken for granted. I needed a starting point. What do we really want from economics? As we gradually figure that out, we can decide the most efficient vocabulary for description and prediction. That's what Newton did. I didn't like the lazy assumption that those problems had already been solved.

Newton lucked out in that old words like mass, force and energy would mostly do if he gave them exact definitions within their usual ranges of meanings. Brand new terms would have made tougher reading, and his *Principia Mathematica* was tough enough in 1687. I had mostly the same luck in the end. But I didn't know that until I had collected textbooks and economic dictionaries, along with most books on economic history I could find, and meanwhile worked out what I thought the right vocabulary ought to be. We pretty well have to solve every section of the jigsaw puzzle at the same time. I'm my father's son, by the way, and balked at the three-figure prices of some of those textbooks, even though I might fork up as much for a bottle of wine.

My ideas on growth theory and capital theory (explaining rates of interest and return) will get plenty of coverage later. It happens I have also taken a lifelong interest in banks and money theory. This book will cover that. Banks and money are part of the story of growth and interest, and anyhow are worth attention in themselves.

Money has been defined elegantly in terms of what we want from it. We want a measure of value and a medium of exchange. The qualities that give those things are "money-ness." Money should be "transportable," for one, in that we don't really want to lug bags of wampum around. It should be stable in value, so that we can contract over the future with least uncertainty. It should have the same value in different places as well as at different times, to minimize the nuisance of conversion. There should be enough of it that shortage doesn't drive us to the clumsiness of barter. It should be "divisible" into tiny units, as hundred-dollar bills into tens and ones and pennies, for exact payment with nothing owed back. It should be fungible in that one unit, say dollar, is worth exactly the same as another. Most essential of all, money should be something actually and reliably valued.

What meets all these criteria? Gold has been a contender since ancient times. But how reliable is its value? Spain and Portugal stockpiled gold and silver from the New World for two centuries, and bought nothing but inflation for their trouble. Gold is good for filling teeth, for coating surfaces with a chemically inert layer, and for displaying status so long as it is rare. Then what is better?

Two brilliant and dangerous adventurers, the Scotsman John Law and the Irishman Richard Cantillon, proposed land. France in 1720 had no New World mines, and needed money. It had plenty of land in Mississippi and Louisiana. Law and Cantillon put two and two together. I think they sincerely believed their advice to The Duke d'Orleans, the regent after the death of Louis XIV, that land could be the most reliable basis of value then known. More than that, I think they were probably right. But it wasn't reliable enough. Early investors in paper rights to the land had made a mint as others crowded in. Market euphoria led to more paper rights than underlying value. You've heard that one before. Law and Cantillon saw the crash coming. It would be called the "Mississippi bubble." Cantillon sold out just in time. Law preferred to face the music, as I would in the Neutral Zone a quarter millennium later. Land wasn't the answer.

I can't call Law and Cantillon good guys like the Emir. Both seem to have committed murder for money, Law long before and Cantillon long after, in scandals in London having nothing to do with the bubble. But they had good days. Cantillon's book, which I know only from descriptions by economic historians, seems to be a masterpiece of the obvious-in-hindsight. Law went down with the ship, like a mensch, and seems to have kept the trust and friendship of many backers he had bankrupted. I mention the plusses of these two men to remind us that the truth is seldom black and white, and to mitigate the folly of the French in trusting them.

Money today, in the United States and elsewhere, is not backed by any commodity. It is "government fiat money" backed by the taxing power of government. That may be the best solution tried so far. The value behind the taxing power is the total capital of the nation, meaning human as well as physical capital. And the dollar has proved pretty stable since Paul Volker's tough reforms in the early 1980s. That means that government fiat money in this county is working about as well as anything we have known.

But there are problems. Government tools for stabilizing government fiat money, which has no value in itself, are limited to control of its supply. The tools are monetary and fiscal policy. Monetary policy is mostly "open market operations" where government sells bonds to soak up excess money, and buys them back again to put money back in the system. You can also raise or lower Central Bank interest rates to get the same effects. Fiscal policy trims money supply by raising taxes and cutting government expense, and pumps money back into people's hands by lowering taxes and raising government expense. Monetary policy is the tool of choice because it has acted must faster. But either policy, or any mix, is a tightrope walk. Too much money courts inflation by motivating people to spend rather than save. Too little courts recession by motivating the opposite. Macro so far has meant the art of walking that tightrope to balance full employment with money value stability. It rests on micro in the sense that it works by manipulating supply of money and demand to invest. But are we wise to push our luck on that tightrope forever?

Another problem is that our current money system may depend too much on banks. Banks buy and sell back the government bonds, for example, and create the money they lend by writing it into the borrower's checking account and booking the promissory note as value received in return. This logic is sound so far. The problem is that banks are failure-prone. I mean plain commercial banks which do nothing but accept deposits and make loans, not the still more dangerous commercial/investment hybrids which rose and fell after repeal of the Glass-Steagle Act.

The danger in ordinary deposit-and-lend banks is leverage. Depositors must be attracted at some cost, say checking services. Borrowers must be attracted at a rate covering those costs. Then equity investors must be attracted at an equity rate, which is generally higher because equity imposes risk. These rates and costs are market givens rather than what the bank decides. Then how can profit from lending rates, watered down by costs of attracting depositors, translate into higher equity rates?

Easily but dangerously. That's where the leverage comes in. If the amount borrowed is much larger than the *amount* invested as equity, absolute profit from borrowing might be large compared to the amount invested. If hens lay only one egg per day, but I own three hens, then I can eat three eggs a day.

More money lent out, compared to equity invested, presupposes more deposits to lend. The leverage needed, or deposit/equity ratio in the bank's case, works out to equal the market equity return for investments of equal risk, divided by the market borrowing rate for loans of such term and risk, net of expense percent including costs of attracting depositors. This has tended to pencil out at about ten to one.

Firms in general are considered risky when leverage (debt/equity for firms) reaches one to one. Four to six is more typical. Not ten to one. Banks invest in loans, which are safer because creditors are paid first and fail last. But not ten times safer. All decks sink when the ship does, and top-heavy ships are asking for it. Few people today would risk their money in bank deposits without federal deposit insurance. My own reading of history finds that deposit-and-lend banks have failed systemically, or needed bailouts, about once per generation since they were innovated in Marco

Polo's time. 2008 gave the worst case, not the first, since the world depression. They failed because borrowers default in high winds, and defaults are magnified tenfold in effects on stockholders' investment. We rebuilt them, and the tenfold leverage, because we blamed the high winds rather than the rickety structure. The Practical Pig knew better.

It began occurring to me in the mid '90s that stock and bond mutual funds might replace bank deposits, and deal with the tightrope problem too. Too much money burns holes in pockets today because money earns nothing while we hold it. Mutual funds pay returns, and are owned for their own sake. If their shares were somehow money, people would feel no impatience to spend it, and no supply would be too much. I gradually figured out how the obvious problems in fungibility and divisibility and other moneyness qualities could be addressed.

Nobelist Franco Modigliani heard of this, and invited me to MIT for a presentation. He talked like Gepetto in Disney's "Pinocchio." There were a few other top brains, including Rudiger Dornbusch and Julio Rotemberg, in the small classroom where I spoke. Sometimes Modigliani interrupted. "Getty, you don'ta consider this." "You forgeta that." I guess I thought I wasn't doing so well.

My talk ended, and he and I were standing by a window. To lighten the mood, I said something about the Red Sox. He said "Getty, I getta papers on banka reform every week. Yours isa the best."

Milton Friedman, another Nobelist, had a different take. We had given talks at a Cato Foundation symposium in San

Francisco. He hated my idea. No great surprise. He had written that money *ought* to earn nothing so that we wouldn't own too much. Any attempt to back money with anything, he told me, would meet John Law's fate in the Mississippi bubble. The backing commodity would become inflated and then crash. So Nobelists can disagree.

My version of the same idea today, which I call "market money," looks first to ETFs (exchange traded funds). ETFs are more liquid and money-like than mutual funds. They are usually fixed portfolios representing broad markets, as with index funds. These need no active management, since they own stakes in market sectors as a whole rather than picking and choosing, and so charge very small expense ratios. Ordinary mutual funds can't match the instant liquidity of ETFs, but might become money too. My idea, dead opposite from Friedman's, is that both money supply and money yield should be held as high as possible.

What would happen to banks? Major angst but not much damage. They would devolve into their separate deposit and lending specialties, with separate stockholders and only incidental interaction. Deposits would be invested in ETFs or mutual funds. Federal deposit insurance would wither away as unneeded. There are no runs on ETFs. Lending banks would have to raise funds to lend from investors expecting a return.

Is there a downside? There is certainly a risk of one. The devil we don't know is what would happen to lending rates and what the consequences might be. That had been one of Modigliani's points in his interruptions. Federal deposit insurance subsidizes cheap money and keeps lending rates low. Most tradition associates easy money with growth and prosperity. Higher interest rates are associated with restraint in investment and consumption both. Modigliani was right to worry.

My guess is that the bank reform and money reform I propose would motivate borrowing costs up, borrowing volume down, and equity investment up to fill the gap. Corporations would issue new stock to retire corporate debt. Newlyweds would rent, not buy, until their incomes were high enough to bring other options.

These concerns are reasons to go slow. I think that the reforms I describe are developing now, with no input from me, and will continue if they succeed. Depositors will be attracted away from banks to ETF accounts of equal liquidity and full return. Federal deposit insurance will not be advantage enough to hold them. Banks will get the message and join the parade by spinning off their loan departments and investing deposits in ETFs. If Modigliani's valid concerns haven't found good answers, the parade will stop until they do. It could backtrack to the starting point. The reforms I believe in ought to work, but can be scrubbed without much mess if they don't.

I am not their only advocate. Others argue for splitting up commercial banks more or less as I would. Meanwhile many people maintain liquidity in ETFs or mutual funds rather than banks. There may be some originality in putting the two reforms together.

This personal account can end with more thoughts about my father. My stepmother Teddy's touching book about their marriage, out a couple of years ago, tells the truth, the whole truth and nothing but the truth. That's what she did throughout her life. He seems not to have been the easiest guy to be married to. He pinched pennies, went on trips while she held up the home front, came home late. My mother had about the same story. But I saw different sides of him at different times and places.

Twice I saw him cry. Once we were listening to a Caruso record. He might well have heard Caruso, although I don't recall that he said so. He would already have been 28 when Caruso last sang at the Met. One of the two books he wrote by himself shows him as an opera buff when on his own in Germany in the 1930s. He wrote what operas he had heard, who sang, and what he liked. My mother said the same. Once they arrived late at a performance of *La Boheme* somewhere on the Riviera, couldn't find a program, liked the tenor, decided to help him, and learned that they had failed to recognize Beniamino Gigli.

The other time was about his and Teddy's son Timmy. Timmy's brain tumor was inoperable and growing. He was 13. The doctors had told them to prepare for the worst. We were in London. The papers said something about young toughs called Teddy boys. My father started crying. Timmy wouldn't make it, and the Teddy boys would.

I've now lost a son myself. You thank the graces for what's left to do. What's left to do includes composing, verse and economics. The first has panned out okay. A fair bit of the verse was set in the music. At least that makes it read and heard. Aside from the kind words of Modigliani and a few others, I can't say as much for my economics. So here goes again.

2

FREE GROWTH THEORY

I dropped the course on economics because I couldn't see the foundations. Not that they should be clear from the start. That isn't how the mind works. We see, do and understand in that order. The pyramids rose four thousand years before people like Galileo and Newton found the laws that made them possible. Practice comes first, and science last. Science is abstraction from the particular to the general. It is fewer rules predicting more outcomes more exactly. The pyramid builders knew rules for this kind of stone and that kind of wood or rope. Newton gave rules for mass and force. Those are not particular things like stone and wood and rope. They are qualities of all things. Their rules are tougher to get our minds around, but predict everywhere once we do.

We will jump in at the deep end. Economics is heavy going. It is a rationale of choices, and choices lie inside. Since we can't see there, we have to figure things out from clues and from what we know in general. That doesn't come naturally. We tend to distrust and resent logic predicting what and how we think. But that's what economics means, and logic and economics are what we signed up for. It will take us to abstractions about abstractions, as in math, with occasional relief in evidence along the way. I gave warning that we will end up in strange places. All the more reason to make sure of every step, and test the logic as best we can while keeping up the pace.

CAPITAL AS PRESENT VALUE

Growth theory begins with understanding capital and output. Capital in principle is anything we will compete to own. We compete to own it because we foresee that it will give the means to satisfy our desires, called "tastes." It might satisfy them directly, as with an ice cream cone, or indirectly as with a dairy or ice cream parlor that will generate other things that generate the cone over time. Economists call the dairy and parlor, and for some economists and laymen like myself the cone too, examples of "physical capital" tradeable in principle. Human capital means our untradeable skill sets. These two are the "factors" of production.

We value things according to what we think their potential benefits are worth now. Anyone who has refinanced a house or cashed in an annuity knows firsthand what present value is. It is also called discounted cash flow, where cash flow to the lender or annuitant is the contractual interest or annuity payments. Present value is the sum of future payments due under the contract, each discounted for time over the remaining period from now to that payment.

Sumerian clay tablets translated by Leonard Wooley in 1929 show that their bankers (temples) used this method, figuring compound interest, to price bonds three thousand years ago. Leonardo Fibonacci published the math in 1225. William Petty in 1664, a century before Adam Smith, realized that the same logic holds for all investment in all economic value, even including the value of our earning power to ourselves. Capital, including that human capital, is valued for the taste satisfactions in consumption that it is expected to yield, discounted for our impatience while we wait, and disappears as the satisfactions arrive. It is as when the bond's value drops by the amount of the current payment. Future value matures into present value when the future becomes the present, and disappears when it becomes the past.

SAVING, INVESTMENT AND PHYSICAL CAPITAL GROWTH

The language of macro, and of growth theory as a part of macro, was set more or less by John Maynard Keynes in his *General Theory*[1] published in 1936. Chapter 6 of that book reasons

output = income,
output = investment + consumption,

---

[1]   *The General Theory of Money, Interest and Employment.*

income = saving + consumption, and therefore
saving = investment.

I call these the "Chapter 6 Equations." They are meant to be understood in two versions; all terms together except consumption can be taken as either gross or net of depreciation. I will mean the net versions unless the context makes the other clear.

Since output means creation of value, and income means rights to that creation, the first equation at least is safe. I call the second the Y=I+C doctrine, or simply the Y doctrine, from the standard notation economists use. Y means output or equivalently income. I will argue that this equation needs adjustments to account for human capital, and is true if we put imaginary asterisks after investment I and consumption C to mean the adjustments. Let's assume for now, anyhow, that the Y doctrine is true as it stands.

Does (net) investment I in that equation mean investment at cost in consumption foregone, or at market realization as new goods are produced and sold? Gunnar Myrdal, writing at about the same time as Keynes, pointed out that the cost of investment in new production, including the cost of time as imputed interest on assets owned, was generally different from the market value realized. Random ups and downs brought sales prices higher or lower than costs. *Ex ante* investment meant the at-cost valuation, and *ex post* the at-market one. I will use "at cost" and "at market," rather than Myrdal's terms, because I am not sure that his meanings and mine are always the same.

Tradition treats cost and market as equal on the assumption that these random differences, which offset in the big picture, are the only ones. Then investment, in the traditional view, means consumption restraint and capital growth equivalently. If so, more of one would imply less of the other after random exceptions cancel. But what about innovation? Productivity gain means more from less. More from less means market realization greater than cost, so that capital growth could speed up without a pause in consumption.

At first this seems impossible. Innovation needs research and development costs that rote replication avoids. Those costs typically saddle innovation with months or years of negative cash flow, meaning money poured in rather than taken out, before new products come to market and cash flow turns from negative to positive. What could pay for that cash flow deficit at the first if not borrowing from consumption?

We see the answer in stock quotes every day. The market estimates all future cash flows, not only the negative ones at the start, along with the discount rate that brings them all to present value. It invests only if it bets that the present value of positive flows later will outweigh the cost of negative ones first. It capitalizes the future as a whole, and funds the early deficit from that newly created wealth.

There is no inflation, and no borrowing from consumption, because the wealth created is real. Markets create wealth simply by thinking it is there. Value is capitalized prediction, and the market shows the consensus where predictions meet. It's actually that simple. Market less cost gives what I call "free growth." Random ups and downs, which Keynes called windfall gain and windfall loss, give its random component. Productivity gain adds a systematic and secular (lasting) one.

The predictions by which markets create wealth are never exact. The market always overvalues some prospects while undervaluing others, and bids prices up and down to correct the mispredictions as events reveal them. A hypothesis that these misguesses offset overall, and apply to all markets rather than to security markets alone, so that all capital growth is this capitalization of the future subject to those offsetting misguesses, can be called free growth theory. I will try to prove that it is correct.

John Stuart Mill saw the free growth possibility in 1848.[2] He wrote:

> There are other cases in which the term saving, with the associations usually belonging to it, does not exactly fit the operation by which capital is increased. If it were said, for instance, that the only way to accelerate the increase of capital is by increase of saving, the idea would probably be suggested of greater abstinence, and increased privation. But it is obvious that whatever increases the productive power of labor creates an additional fund to make savings from, and enables capital to be enlarged not only without additional privation, but concurrently with an increase of personal

---

[2]   *Principles of Political Economy*, Book 1, Chapter 5, Subchapter 4.

consumption. Nevertheless, there is here an increase of saving, in the scientific sense. Though there is more consumed, there is also more spared. There is a greater excess of production over consumption. It is consistent with correctness to call this a greater saving. Though the term is not unobjectionable, there is no other which is not liable to as great objections. To consume less than is produced, is saving; and that is the process by which capital is increased; not necessarily by consuming less, absolutely. We must not allow ourselves to be so much the slaves of words, as to be unable to use the word saving in this sense, without being in danger of forgetting that to increase capital there is another way besides consuming less, namely, to produce more.

This points out that free growth still needs saving. Capital growth arrives for free, but we must first save enough from gross income to make up for depreciation, just as if there were no innovation and no growth, before consuming the rest. Mill says only that we need no more saving in growth, even when growth accelerates, than in staying where we were. Productivity gain, or "whatever increases the productive power of labor," plus market recognition of its potential, does the rest.

Mill allowed for growth by constraint as well. It has been practical to test between the two explanations since national accounts began reporting market-valued capital in 1990 or so, called "net worth of households and foundations" in our own national accounts, and reconstructing it backward several decades further. Consumption has been reported since national accounts first appeared in 1930 or so. My test needs no other data from national accounts; consumption and market-valued capital are enough. Since I'm testing Mill's idea that investment or saving in the sense of realized capital growth needn't be the same as in the sense of consumption deferred, I measure both separately. I begin by specifying (net) investment I in the Y doctrine to mean change in market-valued capital, found as each year's value less the previous year's. That gives the doctrine as

output = capital growth + consumption,

remembering that I really believe this only with the asterisks. Then

capital growth = output − consumption,

showing Mill's point that faster growth can come either from more output or from less consumption.

To make unbiased comparisons among small and large economies, and within the same economy as it grows over time, it is usually best to work with percent rates where larger numerators offset larger denominators. So I divide the variables of the last equation by capital at the start of the year to get

$$\frac{\text{capital growth}}{\text{starting capital}} = \frac{\text{output}}{\text{starting capital}} - \frac{\text{consumption}}{\text{starting capital}}.$$

We are trying to learn about *growth* in these three ratios, not about the ratios themselves. Growth in the first means growth in growth, or acceleration. Then the first is capital acceleration rate, or simply "capital acceleration" for short. The second, or output/capital ratio, has been called "capital productivity." Then let gain in this ratio be called "productivity gain." Since I don't know any standard term for the consumption/capital ratio, and since it is preceded by a minus sign in the equation, and since familiar terms tend to have meanings already, I pick the unusual one "cutback" to mean a drop in that ratio. Then growth in the three ratios in the last equation gives

capital acceleration = productivity gain + cutback.

The plus sign before "cutback" is right because two negatives make a positive.

This equation says exactly what Mill did: we can grow capital either by producing more or by consuming less. We could measure its three terms from national accounts to test his hypothesis at this point. But I take one more step for the sake of clearer presentation in charts and tables. I divide all three variables by capital acceleration to get

$$1 = \frac{\text{productivity gain}}{\text{capital acceleration}} + \frac{\text{cutback}}{\text{capital acceleration}},$$

so that the two possible sources of growth will sum to unity (the number one) in every country and period. I define the ratios to the right of the equal sign as the "free growth index" and "thrift index" to re-express this as

1 = free growth index + thrift index.

I call this the "growth source equation," remembering again that it will adjust to the asterisks. Charts and tables here and at my free website (logicandeconomics.com) show test results. My test measures the free growth and thrift index for each year, but reports only the free growth index in charts and tables since the thrift index is implicitly unity minus that. Charts show the free growth index each year, while tables show its average.

They reveal what they are meant to reveal. If cutback (consumption restraint, growth in investment at cost) equals capital acceleration rate (faster growth of market-valued capital) exactly in any given year, the thrift index in that year will show as unity. If the two tend to equal on average after random ups and downs, as expected by tradition, the thrift index will show as less than unity in years of random ups, where cutback is less than capital acceleration rate, and at more than unity in years of random downs where the opposite is true. It would tend to average unity over cycles, if tradition is right, so that the free growth index would mean the index of the random ups and downs averaging zero. If free growth theory is right, it is the free growth index that will average unity and the thrift index that will average zero. If some but not all growth is free, each index will average something between summing to unity.

DATA SOURCE AND TEST RESULTS

My immediate data source for consumption and market-valued capital was the free Piketty-Zucman website collating national accounts through 2010 in eight countries, all converted to 2010 currency values, and conformed where needed to uniform international standards. Independent research explained at the website has extended the annual data back to 1870 for France, Germany, U.K. and U.S. Australia, Canada, Italy and Japan are reported for the period 1970–2010 only.

The charts and tables show that the free growth index varies around unity wherever measured. The example here shows the free growth index for the United States for the entire period 1870–2010 in three versions. All show occasional spikes up and down, especially in early years when data are reconstructed rather than currently measured. The spikes tend to coincide with near-zero denominators, which can amplify mismeasurements. The first (highest) version shows the index for all years, while the next two apply successively wider screens to exclude years where the denominator was near zero.

This screening actually applies a more rigorous and informative test of free growth theory. The denominator of the free growth index is capital acceleration. Since it is positive when growth speeds up and negative when growth slows down, and magnifies mismeasurements as much when small but negative as small but positive, the term "near-zero" covers both dangers. By excluding years

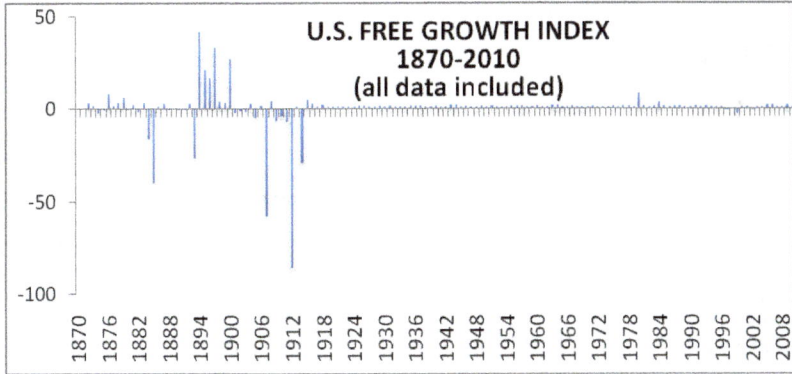

U.S. FREE GROWTH INDEX
1870-2010
(all data included)

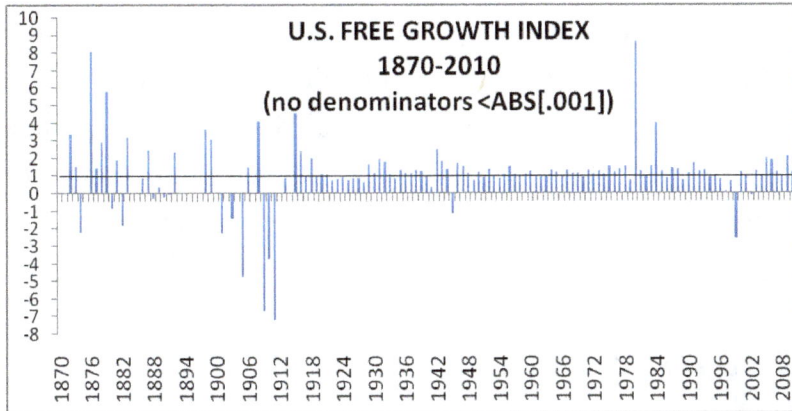

U.S. FREE GROWTH INDEX
1870-2010
(no denominators <ABS[.001])

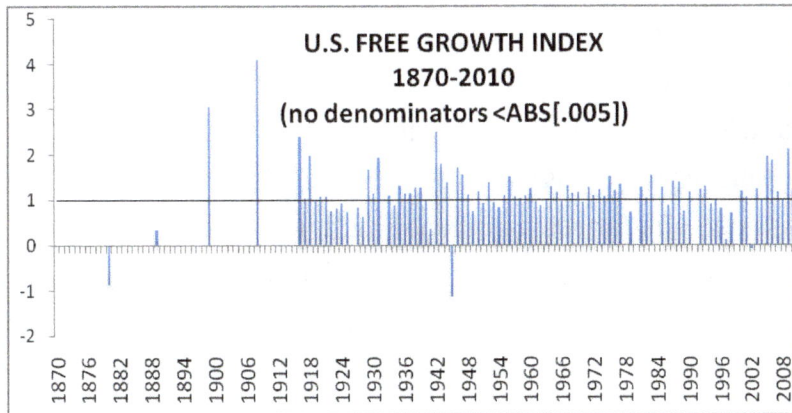

U.S. FREE GROWTH INDEX
1870-2010
(no denominators <ABS[.005])

of near-zero capital acceleration, the test focuses on the sharp accelerations up and down which show the sources of growth least ambiguously. The wider the screen, counterintuitively, the more revealed. What comes through is that free growth is not only possible, but is the only kind reported anywhere. An obvious inference is that the thrift index averages zero by the growth source equation. A subtler one is that although capital acceleration arrives for free, capital replacement to offset depreciation does not. If any part of that tended to be free too, the free growth index would average more than unity. That was Mill's point; we must still save enough to keep capital whole after depreciation.

This summarizes the logic and evidence for free growth theory under the Y doctrine. Now let's see what changes or asterisks that doctrine needs and how the growth source equation adapts.

THE TOTAL RETURN TRUISM

The Y doctrine has found easy acceptance because it seems logical. Output Y means creation of value, and this creation must either add to value of the producing entity or be yielded out. That's why investors prioritize "total return," meaning capital growth plus cash flow. Cash flow is more exactly value yielded out, for reinvestment or gift or exhaust in consumption, less value concurrently invested from outside. Any value growth not explained by cash flow must be explained by current creation. In word equations, the logic is output = value creation,

cash flow = value yielded out – value passed in,

value growth = value creation + value passed in

– value yielded out,

= output – cash flow,   from which

output = value growth + cash flow.

I call this elimination of alternatives the total return truism. Cash flow at the collective scale, where there is no investment from outside and no outlet for yield but exhaust of value in consumption, simplifies to that exhaust. Then the truism at the collective or universal scale becomes

output = value growth + value exhaust.

Now the Y doctrine would follow from the truism if physical capital pure and simple meant value, while investment meant all growth of value and consumption pure and simple meant its exhaust.

But they don't. About three-fourths of all value seems to be human capital, or labor capitalized as present value, to ourselves, of future pay less outside investment in us. This concept, begun by Petty in 1664, became mainstream with work by Theodore Schultz and Jacob Mincer at the University of Chicago in the late 1950s. Schultz realized that not all consumption is exhaust. Some is invested in human capital, just as some dividends from a portfolio are reinvested within the portfolio. This part was what he called "pure investment" of consumption. Only the rest was "pure consumption" exhausted from the economy in satisfying our taste for survival. I rename the first "invested consumption" to distinguish from property investment, since I'll have to talk about both, and follow Schultz on the second. In my words, taken or adapted from Schultz, the idea is

$$\text{consumption} = \text{invested consumption}$$
$$+ \text{pure consumption.}$$

Then the total return truism at the collective scale finds

$$\text{value} = \text{human capital} + \text{physical capital,}$$
$$\text{value exhaust} = \text{pure consumption,}$$
$$\text{output} = \text{value growth} + \text{value exhaust}$$
$$= \text{human capital growth} + \text{physical capital growth}$$
$$+ \text{pure consumption.}$$

Schultz and others also used the term "total capital" to mean the dollar sum of the factors. From now on I will use the terms *value* and *total capital* interchangeably.

THE OUTPUT, PAY AND THREE-FOURTH RULES

The truism alone does not contradict the Y doctrine. If human capital growth were explained entirely by invested consumption, the Y doctrine would be confirmed. But Schultz and modern human capital tradition have argued otherwise. The reasoning can begin with a closer look at the two kinds of consumption.

Schultz saw that invested consumption (his "pure invest-ment") includes schooling plus any other consumption converted into potential for *future* pay, typically through development of strength and skills and soma, rather than enabling *current* pay. That would include schooling and all other consumption before entry in the work force, where physical development is substantially complete and pay begins. Pure consumption, which tends to start at that point, includes a maintenance component adding nothing to future pay, and so adding no new human capital, but meeting the condition for current survival and current pay on which human capital was premised in the first place. No expected maintenance consumption and survival, no expected pay and no present value. This makes invested and maintenance consumption analogous to their counterparts in business accounting; investment builds value for recovery in future cash flow while maintenance and other operating expense perform an expected condition for current cash flow.

The rest of pure consumption, meanwhile, is what Mill and others called "unproductive consumption" supporting neither pay now nor pay later. Not all of these distinctions are explicit in Schultz. We'll see what he said in Chapter 4. Meanwhile the idea is

pure consumption = maintenance consumption
+ unproductive consumption.

The inference that the flow discounted to human capital is pay less invested consumption, in my own terms, has been standard since proposed by William Farr in 1854. Petty had discounted pay without deducting invested consumption. I call this standard view following Farr, which I accept, the human cash flow rule. I may be the first to call pay less invested consumption "human cash flow," but that's what tradition has meant in effect since Farr. Then the human cash flow rule is

human cash flow = pay – invested consumption.

Schultz and Mincer also realized that some work is self-invested, as in the work of learning to complement schooling, and that human capital depreciates as we approach retirement and mortality. These two insights turn out to make the difference between the Y doctrine and the truism. My way of putting the first is

work = self-invested work + realized work,

where "realized" means marketed for pay.

They concluded that human capital growth equals invested consumption plus self-invested work, as the positive components, less human depreciation as the negative one. As this reasoning may have been first published in equation form by Yoram Ben-Porath in 1967, I call it the Ben-Porath equation. In my words, not his, it says

human capital growth = invested consumption
+ self-invested work – human depreciation.

This gives the missing piece in understanding the total return truism. If we shorten "human capital growth" and "physical capital growth" to "human growth" and "physical growth," the truism finds

> output = value growth + pure consumption
>   = physical growth + human growth
>   + pure consumption
>   = physical growth + invested consumption +
>   self-invested work – human depreciation +
>   pure consumption
>   = physical growth + consumption + self-invested
>   work – human depreciation,

by the Ben-Porath equation and the reasoning that consumption equals pure plus invested consumption. Now substitute (net) "investment" for "physical growth" to restate as

> output = investment + consumption + self-invested
>   work – human depreciation,

contradicting the Y doctrine. I call this the output rule.

More becomes clear when we apply the total return truism (output = value growth + cash flow) to human capital separately. It reveals work, the output of human capital, as human growth plus human cash flow at any scale. The Ben-Porath equation and human cash flow rule combine with this to show

51

work = human growth + human cash flow

= invested consumption + self-invested work

– human depreciation + pay – invested consumption

= pay + self-invested work – human depreciation,

from which we get my "pay rule"

pay = work – self-invested work + human depreciation

= realized work + human depreciation.

Comparison between the output and pay rules show that work differs from pay, and collective output from the sum of investment and consumption, each by the same margin between self-invested work and human depreciation. That agreement explains how national accounts, which express both the Y doctrine and an assumption that pay measures work, can find self-consistency. Investment plus consumption are in fact equal to pay plus profit, the output of physical capital, although neither sum gives true output of both kinds of capital together.

We could correct the Y doctrine by substituting either the truism (output = value growth + pure consumption) or the output rule (output = investment + consumption + self-invested work – human depreciation). I prefer the truism as more certain and more tractable. The output rule, but not the truism, assumes that all consumption is either invested in human capital or exhausted in taste satisfaction. Francois Quesnay (pronounced ken-neigh), in Adam Smith's time, argued that workers in manufacturing convert maintenance consumption into products, as a cow turns its fodder into milk. I myself once argued the same. Later I'll show why this hypothesis leads to absurdities. Even so, I cannot refute Quesnay with the finality of the total return truism.

I also find the truism more practical to model in empirical tests. Although human capital and pure consumption are impractical to measure, my "three-fourths rule" estimates them as three-fourths of total capital and all consumption respectively. That would model total capital at four times market-valued capital as reported in national accounts, and pure consumption as three-fourths of all consumption reported there. My estimate of factor proportions as 3:1 parallels the traditional one adopted in something called Cobb-Douglas functions, where typical exponents are three-fourths for labor and one-fourth for physical capital. I fault the underlying logic of those functions, which contradicts the pay rule by equating work to pay, but happen to agree with the conclusion. We'll gradually see why.

Meanwhile I follow Ben-Porath in modeling all consumption before independence as invested. I model all after as pure on the reasoning that invested consumption after physical maturity is limited to adult education, which is real and vital but seems to be rare. If we then suppose that consumption is constant over life, including the imputed cost of parental care in childhood, and that maturity comes at one-fourth of the age of mortality, the three-fourths rule for consumption follows.

Projections of real output by the three-fourths rule cannot be exact. But we can expect that they will come closer than the Y rule does directly. We know at a minimum that total capital is more than physical capital alone, and that pure consumption is less than all consumption. The three-fourths estimate, in both cases, cannot be wildly wrong. Schultz estimated human capital as more than five times physical capital, although that strikes me as high. Farr and others have modeled high invested consumption throughout adulthood, which would contradict my case for the three-fourths rule as to consumption, but I believe all missed the key distinction between investment and maintenance.

That explains the imaginary asterisks. The Y rule becomes exact, at the collective scale, when investment I is re-interpreted as growth of *total* capital and consumption C as *pure* consumption alone.

FREE GROWTH IN STOCK MARKETS

My charts and tables also test free growth theory in stock market data. The counterparts to productivity and the pure consumption /total capital ratio here are total return and dividend rate. Test results are the same as from the national accounts data. The free growth index, meaning change in total return divided by change in growth of market cap, converges everywhere to unity.

MORE ON THE CHARTS AND TABLES

My case for free growth theory rests on the charts and tables shown here and at my website *logicandeconomics.com*. The lollipop-shaped Greek letter φ (*phi*) in them shows the free growth index (productivity gain/capital acceleration rate). $\varphi(K_T)$ shown in red is the version with the asterisks applying the three-fourths rule, and $\varphi(K)$ in blue is the version without. $\varphi(SM)$ in green is the stock market version. We saw that there are spikes, both up and down, which would be expected when inevitable mismeasurement is amplified by near-zero values of the denominator (capital acceleration rate), and that my charts include versions which screen them out. The free growth index clearly jumps around unity, not zero, both before and after the screening. That means that capital acceleration is as likely to coincide with belt-loosening (negative cutback) as belt-tightening (positive cutback).

Now look at Table 1 and the chart tracking the free growth index in Canada. I chose Canada arbitrarily as one of the four countries reporting only forty years of data. That made it practical to show both screen levels along with the unscreened data on a single page.

FREE GROWTH AND CURRENT THINKING

Economists will not be as surprised at the charts and table as they might have been a century ago. Most follow Robert Solow, whose revolutionary papers in 1956 and 1957 founded modern growth theory, in holding that growth is

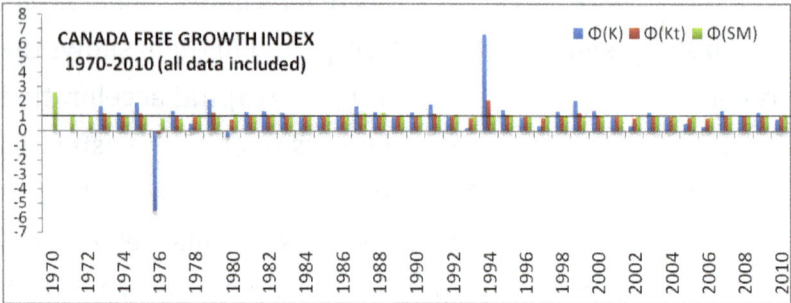

CANADA FREE GROWTH INDEX
1970-2010 (all data included)

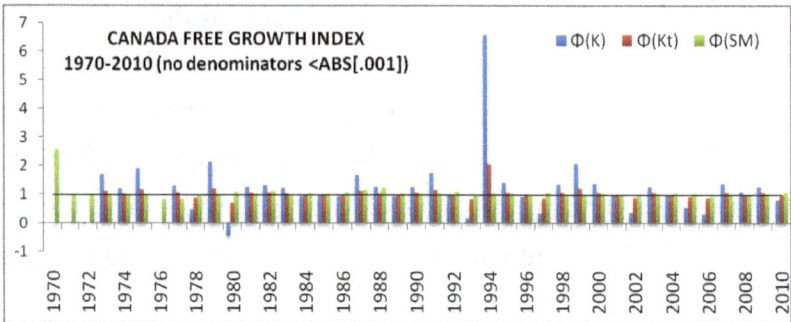

CANADA FREE GROWTH INDEX
1970-2010 (no denominators <ABS[.001])

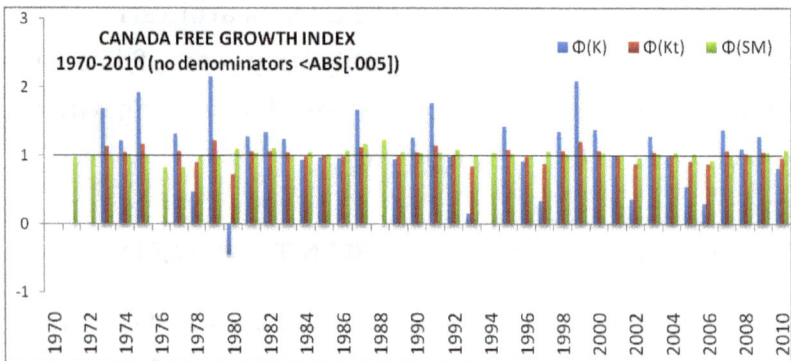

CANADA FREE GROWTH INDEX
1970-2010 (no denominators <ABS[.005])

TABLE 1

FREE GROWTH INDEX (θ=Δr/Δg): ALL COUNTRIES — CORRELATIONS — STOCK MARKETS (Source: GLOBAL FINANCIAL DATA)

Period / Country	Subset	θ(M)	STD. DEV.	MAX	MIN	θ(K)	STD.DEV	MAX	MIN	CQSM	STD.DEV.	MAX	MIN	Ym/K and g(K)	r(T) and g(K)	C/K and g(K)	(SM)	Average*	Std Dev	Maximum	Minimum
1970-2010																					
AUSTRALIA	All Data	0.99	0.20	1.51	-0.06	1.14	1.09	3.74	-4.64	0.60	4.10	0.35		0.71	0.98	0.02	r(SM)	0.08	0.23	0.54	-0.48
	No Dmntrs<ABS(.001)	1.00	0.11	1.51	0.78	1.14	0.59	3.74	-0.19	0.60	4.10	0.35					g(SM)	0.03	0.22	0.47	-0.45
	No Dmntrs<ABS(.005)	1.01	0.06	1.11	0.86	1.05	0.35	1.60	0.25	0.37	2.46	0.35					Div(SM)	0.05	0.02	0.12	0.00
CANADA	All Data	1.01	0.28	2.05	-0.23	1.06	1.06	6.59	-5.56	0.25	2.58	0.83		0.55	0.94	0.16	r(SM)	0.07	0.17	0.33	-0.34
	No Dmntrs<ABS(.001)	1.04	0.20	2.05	0.73	1.06	1.06	6.59	-0.46	0.25	2.58	0.83					g(SM)	0.03	0.16	0.29	-0.37
	No Dmntrs<ABS(.005)	1.02	0.10	1.22	0.73	1.02	0.55	2.16	-0.46	0.07	1.23	0.83					Div(SM)	0.03	0.01	0.06	0.01
FRANCE	All Data	1.25	1.27	9.10	0.45	1.06	6.77	44.18	-1.96	0.29	1.88	-0.16		0.53	0.97	-0.18	r(SM)	0.08	0.26	0.54	-0.41
	No Dmntrs<ABS(.001)	1.05	0.19	1.57	0.45	1.06	0.99	4.02	-1.96	0.29	1.88	-0.16					g(SM)	0.02	0.25	0.51	-0.44
	No Dmntrs<ABS(.005)	1.00	0.12	1.20	0.45	1.06	0.66	2.07	-1.96	0.29	1.88	-0.16					Div(SM)	0.04	0.03	0.14	-0.03
GERMANY	All Data	1.55	3.48	23.08	-0.64	0.95	18.58	118.74	-7.77	0.51	1.47	-2.16		0.52	0.91	0.23	r(SM)	0.10	0.28	1.23	-0.46
	No Dmntrs<ABS(.001)	1.01	0.53	3.11	-0.64	1.02	2.81	12.24	-7.77	0.11	1.47	0.61					g(SM)	0.09	0.28	1.18	-0.47
	No Dmntrs<ABS(.005)	1.02	0.13	1.25	0.55	1.02	0.67	2.31	-1.41	0.11	1.47	0.61					Div(SM)	0.03	0.01	0.05	0.01
ITALY	All Data	1.01	0.27	1.48	-0.32	1.01	1.43	3.55	-6.02	0.45	1.93	-1.55		0.78	0.98	0.46	r(SM)	0.05	0.31	0.90	-0.48
	No Dmntrs<ABS(.001)	1.01	0.27	1.48	-0.32	1.02	1.43	3.55	-6.02	0.45	1.93	-1.55					g(SM)	0.02	0.30	0.82	-0.50
	No Dmntrs<ABS(.005)	1.00	0.11	1.15	0.61	1.01	0.59	1.78	-1.08	0.45	1.93	-1.55					Div(SM)	0.03	0.02	0.08	0.00
JAPAN	All Data	1.04	0.06	1.27	0.95	1.05	0.33	2.42	0.74	0.40	3.32	0.03		0.95	1.00	0.49	r(SM)	0.06	0.27	0.94	-0.42
	No Dmntrs<ABS(.001)	1.04	0.06	1.27	0.95	1.02	0.33	2.42	0.74	0.40	3.32	0.03					g(SM)	0.02	0.27	0.90	-0.42
	No Dmntrs<ABS(.005)	1.03	0.04	1.13	0.96	1.01	0.24	1.71	0.78	0.04	1.23	0.98					Div(SM)	0.01	0.01	0.04	0.00
U.K.	All Data	1.03	0.47	2.91	-0.67	0.99	2.52	11.20	-7.88	0.30	1.49	-0.45		0.80	0.99	0.10	r(SM)	0.09	0.25	1.02	-0.60
	No Dmntrs<ABS(.001)	1.08	0.47	2.91	-0.67	0.99	2.52	11.20	-0.29	0.30	1.49	-0.45					g(SM)	0.04	0.24	0.89	-0.63
	No Dmntrs<ABS(.005)	1.04	0.09	1.28	0.76	0.99	0.48	2.51	-2.57	0.30	1.49	-0.45					Div(SM)	0.05	0.02	0.13	0.01
U.S.	All Data	1.06	0.27	2.43	0.33	1.02	1.44	8.64	-2.57	0.11	1.14	0.42		0.92	1.00	0.27	r(SM)	0.07	0.18	0.34	-0.37
	No Dmntrs<ABS(.001)	1.06	0.27	2.43	0.33	1.02	1.44	8.64	-2.57	0.11	1.14	0.42					g(SM)	0.02	0.17	0.31	-0.39
	No Dmntrs<ABS(.005)	1.02	0.08	1.21	0.80	1.02	0.42	2.10	-0.09	0.11	1.14	0.42					Div(SM)	0.03	0.01	0.06	0.01
1870-2010																					
FRANCE	All Data	1.34	4.11	32.43	-19.39	1.12	21.94	168.61	-107.76	0.40	3.38	-0.16		0.71	0.96	0.38	r(SM)	0.06	0.26	1.47	-0.43
	No Dmntrs<ABS(.001)	1.00	0.58	2.91	-2.77	1.12	3.10	11.18	-19.10	0.40	3.38	-0.16					g(SM)	0.02	0.23	1.26	-0.44
	No Dmntrs<ABS(.005)	1.07	0.26	2.06	0.17	1.12	1.41	6.66	-3.40	0.40	3.38	-0.16					Div(SM)	0.04	0.03	0.21	-0.03
GERMANY	All Data	1.27	2.11	23.08	-0.54	1.11	11.26	118.74	-7.77	0.77	5.34	-2.78		0.74	0.97	0.23	r(SM)	0.05	0.36	1.23	0.00
	No Dmntrs<ABS(.001)	1.02	0.37	3.11	-0.64	1.14	1.95	12.24	-7.77	0.72	5.34	-2.78					g(SM)	0.01	0.34	1.18	0.00
	No Dmntrs<ABS(.005)	1.05	0.18	1.82	0.03	1.17	0.99	5.39	-4.17	0.61	5.34	0.61					Div(SM)	0.04	0.07	0.38	-0.53
U.K.	All Data	1.05	0.70	4.61	-2.62	3.77	3.75	20.25	-18.33	35.84	419.97	-19.43		0.67	0.97	0.09	r(SM)	0.06	0.20	1.02	-1.00
	No Dmntrs<ABS(.001)	1.04	0.33	2.91	-0.67	3.77	1.75	11.20	-7.88	35.84	419.97	-19.43					g(SM)	0.02	0.17	0.89	-0.63
	No Dmntrs<ABS(.005)	1.05	0.11	1.74	0.76	0.98	0.59	4.93	-0.29	4.16	46.25	-8.33					Div(SM)	0.04	0.10	0.34	-0.95
U.S.	All Data	0.94	2.21	8.61	-15.35	1.12	11.77	41.59	-86.20	0.47	2.92	-3.28		0.83	0.99	0.24	r(SM)	0.08	0.19	0.55	-0.38
	No Dmntrs<ABS(.001)	1.02	0.36	2.43	-0.54	0.98	1.91	8.64	-7.20	0.47	2.92	-3.28					g(SM)	0.04	0.18	0.47	-0.42
	No Dmntrs<ABS(.005)	1.03	0.12	1.58	0.60	1.03	0.64	4.09	-1.13	0.21	2.92	0.10					Div(SM)	0.05	0.02	0.08	0.01

θ(M)=Δ(Ym/K/Δg(K)): Change in market-valued output/physical capital rate Ym/K divided by change in physical capital rate g(K).

θ(K)=Δr(T)/Δg(K)): Change in total capital return r(T)=Y(T)-Y(T)/K(T) divided by change in total capital growth rate g(K) is assumed equal to g(K) by the three fourths rule.

θ(SM): Change in stock market total return divided by appreciation. Reproduced directly from Global Financial data.

Ym or Y(M): Consumption C plus market-valued physical growth ΔK.   Yr or Y(T): Pure consumption Cp or C(P) plus total capital growth ΔK(T) or ΔK.   r(T): Total return Y(T)/K(T).

57

mainly exogenous or unexplained by what we sacrifice to spend on it. I cannot do justice to Solow's arguments because they are expressed in the Keynesian language where saving or investment mean their at-cost and at-market versions interchangeably. All growth known so far, at national scales, has proved to be the difference between them. My impression anyhow is that new ideas are seen by Solow to arrive exogenously, meaning costlessly more or less, but that we need to ante up at least something, at least temporarily, to translate them into new capital. Ideas are the free passport to growth, as I interpret Solow, and growth itself the subsidized but not free ticket.

This book, if I have that right, takes the next step in the same direction. The role of thrift is zero. The passport and ticket are both free. It is politicians, not economists, who will be flummoxed. The double tax and the tax preference for capital gains are examples of policies favoring investment over consumption to benefit growth. The record shows no such benefit in any country ever.

FREE GROWTH AND PHILOSOPHY

The truth of free growth theory can be seen in stock market quotes every day. They show that the market adds value as soon as viable innovation is identified, even if years must pass before products come to market and cash flow matures from negative to positive. Saving to offset depreciation, and no more, is always the optimum and is always enough. Even in dislocations as tectonic as the replacement of horses and buggies by automobiles, over the first two decades of the twentieth century, no growth by cutback shows in the data. Saving covered the depreciation of the horses and buggies, just as if they were replaced by new ones without change, and the market paid the cost of the negative cash flows by capitalizing the future.

Something in us resents the fact that the truth in economics is whatever the market thinks it is. We know that thoughts don't make realities in general. If we step from a window in the faith that we can fly, individually or collectively, we will learn otherwise. But economics is a rationale of choices, and choices originate in the mind. Later I will argue that nature put them there, or their guiding principle, and that many classical economists from Petty through Mill taught the same. Whether there is such an ultimate accounting for tastes or not, we can't get far in economics without acknowledging that value is whatever is expected to satisfy them in the future, discounted for the delay.

The fact that buyers and sellers meet at a market-wide price equilibrium is Cantillon's law of one price. It is evidence that predictions and tastes converge, including tastes for impatience defining the discount rate, and that consensus predictions also converge to eventual outcomes, although not so exactly as to preclude buyers from preferring to buy at that equilibrium price, and sellers to sell. With that qualifier, consensus thoughts make market realities. There would be no market, and no economics, if tastes and predictions did not agree enough to allow each buyer to know where to go to find what she wants at a price she is willing to pay, and each seller to rely on enough such buyers to remain in business. These convergence axioms, as I call them, are the founding principles of micro.

The philosopher John Searle, an old friend, points out that words can create objective realities. When the chairman says "the meeting is adjourned," or the pastor says "I now pronounce you man and wife," the words make those things true. In those cases, an established authority speaks the potent words. It is a general consensus of thought, not a pronouncement by empowered authority, that creates reality in the market. Groupthink, or the wisdom of crowds, defines market truth.

We saw how Solow followed different evidence to conclusions something like free growth theory at the same time that Schultz and Mincer were reviving and expanding human capital theory. He puzzled how what he saw could be true. His Nobel Prize acceptance speech at Stockholm in 1988 includes:

> ... In the beginning, I was quite surprised at the relatively minor part the model ascribed to capital formation. Even when this was confirmed by Denison and others, the result seemed contrary to common sense. The fact that the steady-state rate of growth is independent of the investment quota was easy to understand; it only required thinking through the theory. It was harder to feel comfortable with the conclusion that even in the shorter run increased investment would do very little for transitory growth. The transition to a higher equilibrium growth path seemed to offer very little leverage for policy aimed at promoting investment.

The formal model omitted one mechanism whose absence would clearly bias the predictions against investment. That is what I called "embodiment," the fact that much technological progress, maybe most of it, could find its way into actual production only with the use of new and different capital equipment. Therefore the effectiveness of innovation in increasing output would be paced by the rate of gross investment. A policy to increase investment would thus lead not only to higher capital intensity, which might not matter much, but also a faster transfer of new technology into actual production, which would. Steady-state growth would not be affected, but intermediate-run transitions would, and it still does. By 1968 I was able to produce a model that allowed for the embodiment effect. ... If common sense was right, the embodiment model should have fit the facts better than the earlier one. But it did not. Denison (1986), whose judgment I respect, came to the conclusion that there was no explanatory value in the embodiment idea. I do not know if that finding should be described as paradox, but it was at least a puzzle.

Solow is 93 as I write this. He is twice the writer I am, twice the mathematician, and 93 times the economist. What he missed here is the difference between prospective things and their present values. The market sees the new and better products coming, monetizes their present value long in advance, and pays development costs from the proceeds.

The power of the market to create and evaporate value as it likes troubled Keynes. Stock exchanges were necessary evils whose whims, he thought, bore some responsibility for the world depression. Not so. The market is the messenger. Sometimes it garbles and fudges the message, as when little-traded issues show stale (out-of-date) prices, or when sharpsters skew trading or cook the books. Price quotes need not truly *show* what the market thinks. But there is no deeper truth than what it *does* think, and the quotes usually come pretty close. Securities markets give the clearest window on market reality that has yet been devised. Their capitalization of the future to explain free growth will never get the future quite right, as convergence is imprecise, but is as likely to correct upward as downward as events appear.

FINDINGS IN THE OUTPUT LAG METHOD

Some output lag studies seem to support free growth theory, and some to conflict. I would rather trust growth economists to describe the consensus. A 2012 paper by Yin-Wong Cheung, Michael Dooley and Vladyslav Sushko[3] cites five studies between 1961 and 1993 that "find a positive association between investment and growth," meaning output growth, and one each in 2000 and 2006 that find negative or "only marginally statistically significant" association. The authors themselves find positive association in lower-income countries, but negative in higher-income ones.

---

[3]   *Investment and Growth in Rich and Poor Countries.*

How Economists Measure Capital and Its Growth

No one had the data to prove Mill's idea right until national accounts began reporting market-valued capital in 1990 or so, and reconstructing it for a few decades before. What they had earlier was the book measures of capital that we see in balance sheets. This "perpetual inventory method" doesn't reveal enough. Book measures assume depreciation norms. They tell us what assets ought to be worth, from year to year after original construction or purchase, if nothing unusual happened in between. National accounts follow a form of this book or depreciation accounting. They now report market-valued capital too, but still choose book methods, as I said, to calculate investment I and output Y. That doesn't work well. Did you know that national accounts in France, Germany, U.K. and the United States all reported positive net investment in the crash years 1929, 1930, 1937 and 2008? Net investment, meaning net of depreciation, is intended to show growth in capital value. Do you think values really went up in those crash years? And national accounts can be just as wrong in the opposite direction. In the boom year 1933, when stock markets were up 42%, 67%, 96% and 46% in those four countries, Germany and U.S. reported net investment (capital growth) as negative while France and U.K. reported it up less than half a percent. All this shows in my charts and tables.

Reports of net investment in national accounts tend to prove radically wrong in periods of unexpected upturn or downturn because they don't get the news of war or peace or disasters or inventions or slumps or recoveries until new assets are bought and new products sold. Purchases and sales and other cash-flow entries are normally the only input into the books. For all physical capital together, time between looking for assets and recovery in cash flow runs several years. Accounts in those slump years were reporting the good news of boom years shortly before, including the booms of 1935 as well as 1933 preceding the slump year 1937. Accounts in the boom year 1933, incidentally the year I was born, were finally getting the news of the crash. (Yes, some of the strongest boom years in history came during the world depression.)

MARKET-VALUED NET INVESTMENT AND NET OUTPUT

I suggest that national accounts should show (net) investment I and (net) output Y both ways. They should continue to report I and Y by the old perpetual inventory ("book") method for several good reasons, including the fact that not everyone will agree that market measures are more reliable. I mentioned that Keynes himself, a lively writer, contrasted the fickleness of markets to the sober discipline of accounting. But national accounts can now show net investment as change in market-valued capital too. They can then add that difference to consumption to find net product $Y = I + C$ by market rather than book measures as I do. They can publish both book and market versions of I and Y, and let each economist choose.

FREE GROWTH AND FREE GOODS

"Free goods" and "free bads" mean the same as Keynes' random windfall gain and windfall loss. All are neglected in economics as offsetting and unpredictable. Free growth is no such thing. It is secular, not random. It is predicted in that we predict national growth, whether or not realizing that it is free. Its cause is better ideas recognized and capitalized by markets. The challenge to economists is to understand that causality better, and to bring it within the reach of management and policy where they can.

SUMMARY

I promised a heavy slog toward surprise. One surprise was that the Y doctrine, accepted everywhere, misses human capital. It becomes correct when we put imaginary asterisks after investment I and consumption C. (Net) investment must mean total capital growth, and consumption must mean only Schultz's "pure" kind net of invested consumption. Here my argument combined the Ben-Porath equation generally accepted in human capital economics, the total return truism axiomatic in finance economics, and my generalization of the latter to human and total capital. My charts and tables include tests under the assumption $Y = I + C$, even so, as human capital and pure consumption are impractical to measure. But I measure (net) investment at change in market-valued capital reported at the Piketty-Zucman website, not at change in book value as shown in national accounts. I then model in the asterisks with the three-fourths rule: total capital growth should run something near four times market-valued capital growth, while pure consumption should run something near three-fourths of all consumption.

I test Mill's hypothesis that output growth can precede and explain capital growth. First I derive the free growth index as productivity gain/capital acceleration rate, and the thrift index as cutback/capital acceleration rate, where cutback is change in consumption/capital times minus one. The growth-source equation shows that these are complements summing to unity. Data in my charts and tables show that that free growth index converges to unity, and the thrift index by implication to zero, wherever and whenever tested. Output-driven capital growth, which I call free growth, is the only kind observed at national scales.

NOTATION

Mathophobes are free to skip this section, as I hope to have made my point in words and word equations. The same goes for notation in later chapters.

CAPITAL

Let value V and total capital K_T mean the same. The present value rule is

$$V = \int_0^\infty F(t)e^{-\delta t}dt ,$$ (2.1)

Where F is cash flow and δ (delta) is discount or time preference rate. Also

$$V = K_T = H + K = \int_0^\infty F_H(t)e^{-\delta_H t}dt + \int_0^\infty F_K(t)e^{-\delta_K t}dt, \quad (2.2)$$

where H and K are human and physical capital, F_H and F_K are their cash flows, and δ_H and δ_K are their time preference rates.

OUTPUT

Output Y means creation of value. It can be defined implicitly in the truism

$$\dot{V} = Y + F_- - F_+ \,,$$

where negative cash flow F_- means value inserted (invested) from outside and positive cash flow F_+ means value withdrawn.

Now the fact

$$F = F_+ - F_- \tag{2.3}$$

allows the total return truism

$$\dot{V} = Y - F \quad \text{or} \quad Y = \dot{V} + F. \tag{2.4}$$

For the factors, the truism becomes

$$W = \dot{H} + F_H \quad \text{and} \quad P = \dot{K} + F_K \tag{2.5}$$

where work W and (net) profit P are the factor outputs.

CASH FLOW

Positive cash flow in general is reinvestment in different assets of the source individual, or gift to another individual, or exhaust in pure consumption. At the scale of the total capital of an individual, reinvestment cancels internally to leave

$$F_+ = \gamma_+ + C_p,$$

where γ_+ is gift and C_p is pure consumption. Meanwhile the only means of negative cash flow at that scale is gift received γ_-. Define net gift γ by $\gamma = \gamma_+ - \gamma_-$ to reach

$$F = F_+ - F_- = \gamma_+ + C_p - \gamma_- = \gamma + C_p \tag{2.6}$$

at the individual scale. At the collective or universal scale, net gift γ also cancels internally. That leaves

$$F = C_p \quad \text{at the collective scale.} \tag{2.7}$$

THE OUTPUT RULE

What I call the Ben-Porath equation is equation (4) in his 1967 paper, summarizing the first three. In my words and notation, rather than his, it shows

$$\dot{H} = C_s + W_s - D_H \qquad (2.8)$$

where C_s is Schultz's invested consumption, W_s is his self-invested work, and D_H is his human depreciation.

By this and the total return truism at the collective scale,

$$Y = \dot{V} + C_p = \dot{H} + \dot{K} + C_p = C_s + W_s - D_H + \dot{K} + C_p$$

which simplifies to

$$Y = \dot{K} + C + W_s - D_H \qquad (2.9)$$

if consumption C equals C_s plus C_p. This contradicts the Y doctrine $Y = I + C = \dot{K} + C$.

THE GROWTH SOURCE EQUATION

Since my charts and tables derive the growth-source equation from the Y doctrine with and without the asterisks, I'll show it both ways here too. The version $Y = I + C$ without them, substituting $\dot{K}$ for I, can be arranged as $\dot{K} = Y - C$. Divide by K for

$$\frac{\dot{K}}{K} = \frac{Y}{K} + \frac{C}{K}.$$

Define physical growth rate g_K, proxy productivity y_K and consumption rate c_K by

$$g_K = \frac{\dot{K}}{K}, \quad y_K = \frac{Y}{K} \quad \text{and} \quad c_K = \frac{C}{K}$$

to re-express this as

$$g_K = y_K - c_K, \quad \text{implying} \quad \dot{g}_K = \dot{y}_K - \dot{c}_K.$$

Let $\dot{y}_K$ be called proxy productivity gain, and let $-\dot{c}_K$ be called "physical cutback." $\dot{g}_K$ is "physical acceleration rate." Divide by $\dot{g}_K$ and rearrange for

$$\frac{\dot{y}_K}{\dot{g}_K} - \frac{\dot{c}_K}{\dot{g}_K} = 1. \tag{2.10}$$

Define free growth index $\varphi(K)$ (φ is *phi*) and thrift index $\theta(K)$ (θ is *theta*) as $\dot{y}_K / \dot{g}_K$ and $-\dot{c}_K / \dot{g}_K$ respectively. That allows (2.10) to be re-expressed as

$$\varphi(K) + \theta(K) = 1. \tag{2.10a}$$

Now comes the version with the asterisks that I believe. The total return truism $Y = \dot{V} + C_p$ at the collective scale, can be arranged as $\dot{V} = Y - C_p$. Divide by V for

$$\frac{\dot{V}}{V} = \frac{Y}{V} - \frac{C_p}{V}. \quad \text{Let this show as}$$

$$g = r - c_p, \quad \text{implying} \quad \dot{g} = \dot{r} - \dot{c}_p$$

where g is growth rate of total capital, r is its rate of return or productivity, $\dot{g}$ is its acceleration rate, $\dot{r}$ is its "productivity gain," c_p is pure consumption rate, and $-\dot{c}_p$ is cutback in the total capital sense. Division by $\dot{g}$ gives

$$\frac{\dot{r}}{\dot{g}} - \frac{\dot{c}_p}{\dot{g}} = 1. \quad \text{Express as} \quad \varphi(V) + \theta(V) = 1, \qquad (2.11)$$

where $\varphi(V) = \dfrac{\dot{r}}{\dot{g}}$ and $\theta(V) = -\dfrac{\dot{c}}{\dot{g}}$ are the free growth and thrift indexes in that full sense.

THE THREE-FOURTHS RULE

My three-fourths rule first estimates

$$H \to .75K_T \quad \text{and} \quad C_p \to .75C.$$

That first estimate and the definition $H + K = K_T = V$ combine for

$$V = K_T \to 4K.$$

Given a simplifying assumption that K / K_T holds constant, this allows

$$\dot{V} = \dot{K}_T = 4\dot{K}.$$

Thus the three-fourths rule projects

$$Y = \dot{V} + C_p = \dot{K}_T + C_p = 4\dot{K} + .75C. \qquad (2.12)$$

Further, consumption rate C_p in the total capital sense is modeled as

$$c_p = \frac{C_p}{V} = \frac{.75C}{4K} = \left(\frac{3}{16}\right)\frac{C}{K} = \frac{3}{16}c_K,$$

So that cutback in the two senses compare as

$$-\dot{c}_p = -\frac{3}{16}\dot{c}_K.$$

The two versions of the thrift index show

$$\theta(V) = \frac{-\dot{c}_p}{\dot{g}} \text{ and } \theta(K) = \frac{-\dot{c}_K}{\dot{g}_K}.$$

By the assumed constant 4:1 proportionality of V or K_T to K, K_T and K are modeled as agreeing throughout in growth and acceleration rates. Now

$$\theta(V) = \frac{-\dot{c}_p}{\dot{g}} = \frac{3}{16}\left(\frac{-c_K}{g_K}\right) = \frac{3}{16}\left(\frac{-\dot{c}_K}{\dot{g}_K}\right) = \frac{3}{16}\theta(K). \qquad (2.13)$$

My charts and tables show free growth indexes $\varphi(V) = 1 - \theta(V)$ and $\varphi(K) = 1 - \theta(K)$ rather than thrift indexes directly. The free growth indexes compare as

$$\varphi(V) = 1 - \theta(V) = 1 - \frac{3}{16}\theta(K) = 1 - \frac{3}{16}\Big[1 - \varphi(K)\Big]$$

$$= 1 - \frac{3}{16} + \frac{3}{16}\varphi(K) = \frac{13}{16} + \frac{3}{16}\varphi(K). \qquad (2.14)$$

This reveals why $\varphi(V)$ fluctuates much nearer unity in the charts and tables than does $\varphi(K)$. If we could somehow measure $\varphi(V)$ directly, rather than estimate it in the three-fourths rule, we would still see a tighter variance in $\varphi(V)$. The ratio C_p/V will not hold at steady $\frac{3}{16}$ of $\frac{C}{K}$, in the real world but it will run in something near that range by the facts that C_p is less than C while K is substantially less than V.

3

DEPRECIATION, RISK AND MORE ON THE PAY RULE

This book would have been shorter, and easier to write and read, if I accepted the Y doctrine as all authorities seem to do. Free growth theory would have been simpler to explain, and about as well supported in the charts and tables. That and next generation theory and my macro ideas outlined in Chapter 1 would have been plenty to fit into one book. None of them needs the asterisks by which I turn the Y doctrine into the output rule. I suppose I could have stuck to those themes, and left out the asterisks in good conscience as irrelevant.

But here we are. The output rule and pay rule probably rank with free growth and next generation theories as the biggest of the surprises promised in my title. My risk theory and depreciation theory, which hold surprise in their own right, help prepare the way for them and will be taken first.

DEPRECIATION THEORY

I define depreciation as recovery of investment in revenue and cash flow.[1] Depreciation in a wider sense also includes deadweight loss, meaning investment lost from total capital but not recovered in cash flow. Economists use depreciation in both senses. I use the narrower one excluding deadweight loss, and call the wider one "decapitalization" to tell them apart. Economic dictionaries show depreciation as loss of value due to deterioration or obsolescence with age. They miss the point. Value is discounted cash flow. Cash flow recovers investment plus realized profit. Assets depreciate (lose value) by the amount of recovered investment, but not by realized output, because output by definition is value newly created rather than drawn from capital in place. Depreciation is investment recovery at bottom. We will see that it is loosely connected to deterioration and obsolescence, but need not imply either.

How do we tell these output and depreciation components of cash flow apart? Accounting tradition usually depreciates from original cost in a straight line over standard depreciation periods. National accounts, and some firms, have found refinements. Current cost accounting, for example, corrects distortions due to past inflation when we book assets in dollars of the date of purchase or construction, years or decades ago, and then depreciate from that

---

[1] More precisely in gross realized output, or positive cash flow plus plowback for recovery with interest later. All depreciation is recovered eventually, if not concurrently, in cash flow. This will be detailed in the next chapter.

base as the value of the dollar changes. If a building cost $500,000 in 2000 and was expected to last 50 years, for example, simple linear depreciation from that point will show it as worth $400,000 in 2010 and $300,000 in 2020.

But dollars of 2000, 2010 and 2020 may not agree in purchasing power. Current cost accounting adjusts that original cost ($500,000) to the equivalent in today's dollars, and then depreciates linearly or otherwise from that updated starting value over the same original asset lifespan. Remaining asset value shows as higher if the dollar is worth less now, but so does current depreciation because it divides a higher starting value by the same number of years. If the dollar has deflated instead, meaning that it is now worth more, both remaining value and current depreciation show as less. The advantage of showing things that way is to reveal all information in the books by the same current dollar standard. This is a big step forward.

National accounts adopt this method, and also apply "declining balance" depreciation to replace linear depreciation with a curve believed more realistic. I will try to prove that they are right in faulting straight-line depreciation, but that they correct it in the wrong direction. They rely on records of actual sales of structures and durables to model loss of value as steep initially and slower later. Most value would be lost early, and gradually less later, as in pouring honey from a jar. I suggest that a relatively few distress sales bias this record, and that the truth beneath is exactly the opposite.

My argument, like my definition of depreciation, works from the principle that all capital is discounted cash flow as buyers appraise future benefits, consciously or unconsciously, and discount for the delay. Experience shows that they tend to like durable assets that provide the same benefit or service or "utility" every day, and that markets tend to meet that demand. Utility is expressed in cash flow. Evidence in office or apartment rents or taxi fares, for example, shows that reasonably steady cash flow over asset life, inflation-adjusted, is a realistic and normal assumption. Say then that a given long-term asset is expected to depreciate over 50 years, as more or less with human capital or buildings, and that cash flow is expected to be constant. Also suppose a constant time-discount rate. Present value at the outset is 50 years of discounted cash flow.

At the beginning of the second year, it is 49 years of present value of the same cash flow discounted at the same rate. All that has been lost is present value of the 50th or most distant year. It was least in present value among the 50 because the same cash flow was discounted at the same rate over the longest period. At the start of the third year, capital has dropped again by present value of the 49th and second-most distant and discounted year. So it continues until the end as the discount period approaches zero. Value loss *increases* absolutely each year, and increases even faster in ratio to shrinking capital, because each yearly decrement in overall present value is more than the one before.

What I just modeled is value loss, meaning depreciation if nothing new is invested, rising exponentially from negligibility at the start to a maximum at the end. National accounts show the exact opposite. They show it decreasing exponentially from a maximum at the start, because that is what the evidence proves when we sell unexpectedly. When we sell a car soon after buying it, we take a big hit. It's the same when a company buys or builds a plant to operate it, but changes its mind soon after and sells. The market into which they sell worries what went wrong. Was the car a lemon? Did the first owner misuse it? Is he selling because he knows something about it that I don't know? The company reselling the plant faces these questions and more. Most plant is customized to the operator's business plan. No one else's needs will be quite the same. The buyer will have to discount for the due diligence cost first and a remodeling cost after that.

A thought experiment adds another critique. If declining-balance depreciation were realistic, so that depreciation begins at a maximum and declines exponentially, then the reasonably steady cash flows we seem to witness in rental and lease of buildings and vehicles and other durables would have to be explained by gains in the realized output component of cash flow. Yet the capital generating all output, as present value of all these steady cash flows remaining, must shrink steadily to zero. Both would be possible only if the time-discount rate rose too, contradicting assumptions, and reached infinity at the end. I'll return to this theme.

I suggest that national accounts should continue tracking actual sales as an indicator of true depreciation curves, but should screen out most distress sales by limiting the study to rental buildings expected from the start to be resold several times. I mean apartment buildings, office buildings and warehouses designed along standard lines. Many investors specialize in buying and selling these tradable assets for portfolio purposes. Pressure to buy them and pressure to sell them tend to balance.

My inference that value loss tends to rise rather than fall with asset age can be called the depreciation rule. It contradicts only a minor feature of the national accounts. But it contradicts that diametrically. It is also original as far as I know. Who has said such a thing before? All the more fun and satisfaction in finding out and setting the record straight. There are giants out there, whether I ever make it to their shoulders or not, and economic history means identifying them.

A MORTGAGE ANALOGY

Depreciation theory, meaning that rule and whatever else can be reasoned about depreciation, says that cash flow over asset lifespan follows the same logic as with level payments over the period of a declining-balance mortgage. Mortgage payments are partly amortization and partly interest. Amortization is like depreciation, and interest is like cash flow yielded by the asset. The declining balance is like asset value. Mortgage payments are almost all interest at the start of the loan, when the declining balance on which interest is paid is almost the whole loan amount, and then gradually less interest and more amortization as the interest-earning balance shrinks. As the balance approaches zero at the end, the payment approaches all amortization while the interest share approaches zero.

The key point is that the interest share of the payment is calculated first, as the contractual interest rate times the declining balance, so that amortization is whatever is left. Depreciation theory reasons that the same tends to be true of capital. It need not be so in individual cases because rate of return, the counterpart to interest rate, is a current norm rather than a contractual constant. In the big picture, however, where outcomes converge to norms, the parallel holds.

RISK THEORY AND THE OWNER RULE

For practical purposes, economic risk is usually interpreted as standard deviation (a measure of volatility) in expected rate of return. Although downside risk is what we really worry about, standard deviation means volatility in both directions around the amount expected. Safer assets are expected to vary less. Short-term treasuries are judged safest because they combine fixed return with fast liquidity in case inflation threatens. The market overall bids safer assets up, in proportion to expected output norms, and riskier ones down. Since asset value is the denominator in rate of return, and output the numerator, the effect is make riskier assets higher in return.

Risk tolerance might be anything in any individual. As a norm, it tends to be a function of age, gender and wealth.

Effects of age and gender are better understood. Teens and young adults, particularly males, seem readiest to take chances. Prison admissions and Medal of Honor rolls feature young males. Part of the explanation, I think, is shown in biologist R. A. Fisher's sex ratio theory of 1930, or equally Bob Trivers's differential investment theory of 1971. Young males show greatest variance in reproductive prospects. Females are almost always assured of a few offspring. Young males might eventually leave none or many. Nature arranges tournaments or displays to give fitter males a chance to prove it. Sporting contests, or displays in singing or dancing, are harmless ways to prove male fitness. Crime and war are the dark side. Meanwhile the young, of either sex, have most time left to outride downswings. The older we get, the more risk-averse.

My approach considers risk in both factors, meaning human as well as physical capital, and focuses first on the owner. The guiding principle I follow is that we each choose or adapt capital of both factors to fit our own current risk tolerance.

This individual risk tailoring is axiomatic in professional portfolio management, as is the general rule that most people become more risk-averse with age. Security portfolios are diversified into equities (stocks) and bonds, to guard against inflation as well as business risk, and the ratio is targeted to the investor's risk profile. Most of us, not me, tend to prefer a higher bond/equity ratio as we age. As securities tend to be liquid, meaning tradeable at will and at little cost in stock or bond markets, managers can maintain the current target ratio easily when markets change security values.

We don't have so much flexibility to swap our other belongings, particularly costly and customized ones such as houses and other buildings, and none at all to swap our human capital. But we can adapt these things to suit current risk tolerance instead. Risk lovers can mortgage their homes and other buildings, while risk haters can pay the mortgage down. Human capital too is adaptable. Our skill sets are what they are, at a given age, but we can usually choose among higher and lower risk/reward opportunities for them. Bernie Madoff, who I never met, thank gosh, traded a humdrum career for billions and a life sentence in Ponzi schemes. A fighter pilot trades combat pay for safety when he takes a desk job instead.

It follows that we need only observe the risk-adjusted return of a person's security portfolio to guess the risk and return to all her other assets including human capital. All should agree. A person's risk appetite will change with age and circumstances, but is only one thing here and now. She buys or adapts to suit it. Call this principle the owner rule. It will prove important in defending the pay rule.

It has an inference that is not obvious. Human capital is owned disproportionately by the young. We own very little physical capital, legally or in practical effect, until maturity. Pay at first is barely enough for survival. We accumulate it gradually as pay rises with age, and then deplete it in provision for the young and for our own retirement. Since physical capital is owned disproportionately by the older and more risk-averse, and human capital by the younger and more risk-prone, including young adults, the owner rule predicts human capital to be higher on average in risk and return than physical capital at the scale of all owners together.

THE PAY RULE

SOLVING THE AGE-WAGE PUZZLE

I can approach the pay rule by showing something that troubled Ben-Porath and has troubled many economists since. I call it the age-wage puzzle. Age-wage profiles, mentioned in the last chapter, are published reports comparing pay earned by all working ages at the same time. They might show average pay currently earned by those between the ages of 15 and 25, say, next to pay to the 26–35 bracket, and then to the 36–45 bracket, and so forth through retirement. Since all cohorts (same-age sets) are compared at once, as in a family portrait, age-wage profiles do not show effects of technological growth over time.

They show differences in age and skills at a single moment. Here I offer examples from five nations including ours. What appears is that older cohorts out-earn younger ones until retirement or near it. Meanwhile human capital is the present value of remaining lifetime pay less invested consumption, and it shrinks steadily as approaching retirement, and mortality leaves fewer future paydays to discount. The puzzle is how pay could hold steady or even rise while human capital shrinks smoothly to zero.

Age Wage Profiles in Percent of Wage of Youngest Earners Shown

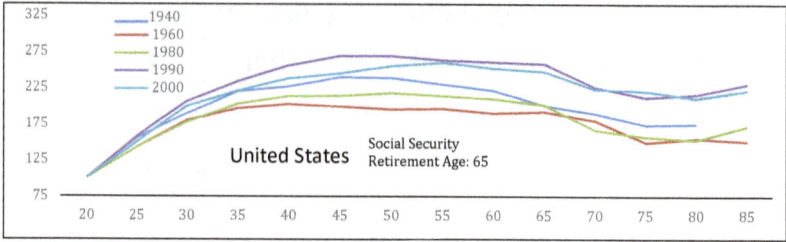

United States — Social Security Retirement Age: 65
Legend: 1940, 1960, 1980, 1990, 2000

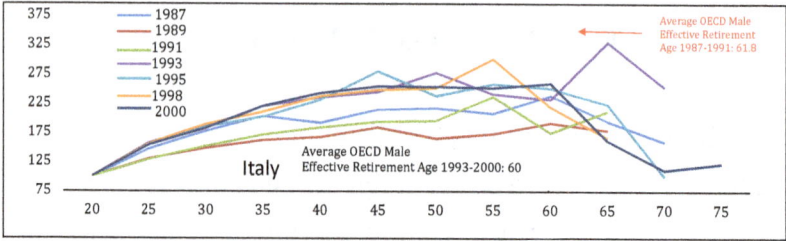

Italy — Average OECD Male Effective Retirement Age 1993-2000: 60
Average OECD Male Effective Retirement Age 1987-1991: 61.8
Legend: 1987, 1989, 1991, 1993, 1995, 1998, 2000

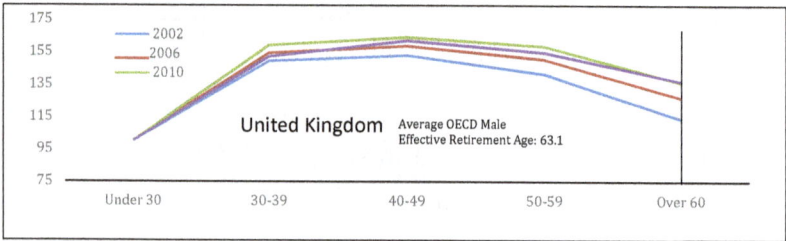

United Kingdom — Average OECD Male Effective Retirement Age: 63.1
Legend: 2002, 2006, 2010

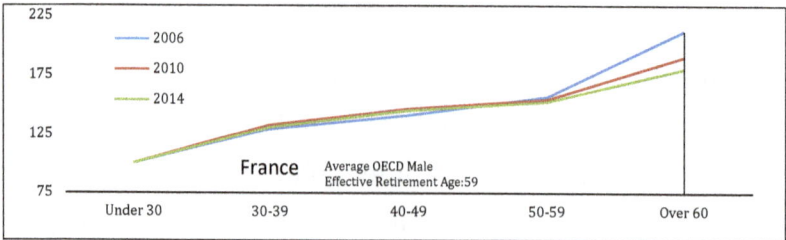

France — Average OECD Male Effective Retirement Age: 59
Legend: 2006, 2010, 2014

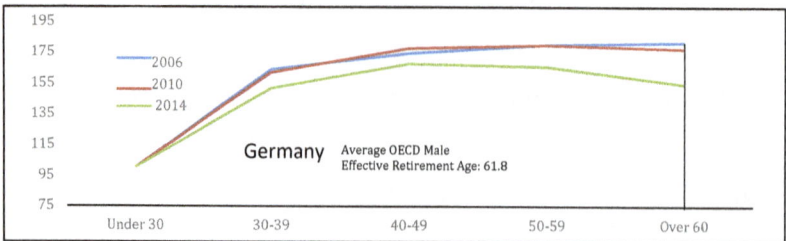

Germany — Average OECD Male Effective Retirement Age: 61.8
Legend: 2006, 2010, 2014

There would be no puzzle if we were talking about the cab fare or office or apartment rents, which seem to hold steady rather than fall over time. Cab fare and rent show the *revenue* of cabs and buildings. Revenue recovers costs including depreciation. Cash flow as I define it deducts costs aside from depreciation, and then also deducts plowback from revenue and new investment from outside. The depreciation rule and the mortgage analogy showed how rising depreciation or amortization can make up for declining output to keep revenue and cash flow steady.

We are puzzled because pay is taught to measure work alone, or more exactly work sold in the marketplace rather than self-invested. Work is defined as the *output* of human capital. Output, in the net sense I use in this book, is creation or value added after costs including depreciation are deducted. Steady or rising work by steadily declining human capital would imply exponentially rising output/capital ratio or productivity, and rising to infinity at the end.

Think about it. Human capital, as present value of future pay less future invested consumption, is at most the present value of expected remaining lifetime pay at current age. (It is even less as long as invested consumption continues.) When only a year of pay is left ahead of us, human capital at most is time-discounted present value of one year's pay. With a day left, it is at most the present value of a day's pay. It follows that if pay were made up wholly of output, rate of return (output/capital) to human capital would be at least 100% per year at the beginning of the last year, then 100% per day at the beginning of the last day, and infinite at the end of the last second. Yet portfolio choices show appetite for risk and return as *declining* with age, and risk theory argues that return to human capital should follow suit.

The thought experiment shown this way can be called the "last day paradox." Here it illustrates and resolves the age-wage puzzle; pay recovers human depreciation.

FURTHER PROOF

Gary Becker, who figured with his teacher Mincer alongside Schultz in the consensus leading to the Ben-Porath equation, hinted at what I call the pay rule in 1964. He pointed out that job training at the employers' expense is part of investment in human capital, and reasoned that employers won't pay it unless they expect eventual recovery with interest. The pay rule pushes this logic to its conclusion. What Becker said holds for any investment in anything by anyone. When we invest for our own benefit, we expect recovery by ourselves. When we invest for the sake of others, we expect recovery by them. Recovery means recovery of depreciation. The depreciation rule and mortgage analogy showed investment recovery as following rather than preceding realized output, against tradition and intuition, but showed that aggregate cash flow over asset lifespan must recover aggregate investment before output is left as the residue. Our parents would not have invested in our human capital without expected recovery of our human depreciation by us, because then nothing would be recovered by anyone, and the young invest the work of learning in themselves because they expect that to be recovered with interest as well. No expected recovery, no investment. Pay recovers human depreciation as an expected norm, just as with a firm's depreciation, because no one would invest otherwise.

There is a variant of this proof which I call the deadweight loss rule. Capital of any kind is present value of cash flow, meaning expected realization in transfer or taste satisfaction. Deadweight loss, as when a house is flooded or human capital is hit by a bus, means decapitalization with neither. It follows that deadweight loss, although a common reality, is implicitly unexpected. But human depreciation, like plant depreciation, is expected from first investment. No one would argue with a straight face that our aging and mortality come as a surprise to ourselves or our parents or theirs or anyone before. That makes human depreciation expected as cash flow by elimination of alternatives.

COMPLETING THE PAY RULE

Each proof of expected recovery of human depreciation is sufficient. The logic that no one would invest without expected recovery expresses what I call the "maximand" rule: we maximize risk-adjusted rate of return. Robert Turgot observed this in 1766. The reason can be seen intuitively. Output is cash flow, which is available to satisfy tastes now, plus growth in total capital. Total capital is present value of foreseen cash flows available for future taste satisfactions, discounted at our own risk-adjusted time preference rate. Tastes are defined as whatever behavior reveals in that prospective as well as current sense. Our whole means of behavior is our skills and possessions in total capital. Then behavior maximizes the ratio of risk-adjusted output to total capital, or equivalently risk-adjusted rate of return.

It takes little thought to realize that maximizing risk-adjusted return presupposes recovery of investment, and that this means recovery of depreciation or amortization. The solution to the age-wage puzzle is that pay does not equal and compensate realized work alone. It compensates that plus human depreciation. The conclusion that human depreciation is recovered in revenue and cash flow can be called the recovery rule.

The pay rule is not entirely certainty, as the recovery rule itself is, because it depends on an assumption that nothing *further* is recovered in pay. We'll get to that soon. It joins free growth theory and the output rule as major examples of the surprises promised in my title. Recovery of human depreciation in pay changes a lot of equations. It does not impact public policy and tax laws as radically as free growth theory, but we will see that it impacts them enough. Even if it didn't, it is probably the most startling assertion in this book from an economist's viewpoint.

And although I now know better than to claim originality for any idea in economics, this one along with depreciation theory just might pass the test. If someone out there knows a precedent closer than Becker's, as I eventually found ones for what I had thought were my own free growth and next generation theories, all the more fun in finding those unsuspected precursors. (Next generation theory will be outlined later.)

I will add a few more proofs that human depreciation is recovered as we go. It is never overkill to drive another stake through the heart of entrenched misperception. We can be as sure of recovery as that two and two make four. The arguments from the maximand rule (Turgot's insight) and the deadweight-loss rule are unanswerable.

WHAT I THOUGHT ONCE

Now we come to the uncertain assumption on which the pay rule depends along with the certainty of the recovery rule. It is opposite from one I made to explain the same evidence in age-wage profiles until a few years ago. I will show how I reasoned then, and how I came to reverse my view.

That can start with comparison of accounting for human capital to accounting for a firm. Pay, in this analogy, is the worker's revenue. The firm deducts outside operating costs of labor and supplies to leave gross realized output. The analogy for human capital would be maintenance consumption enabling life and activity. What I thought then was that human capital expenses this cost as the firm does. It seemed to me that we recover this operating expense in pay and work products, just as the fodder of a cow or stable horse is recovered in milk prices and riding fees. I found out that Quesnay, and a group he led called the physiocrats, could be interpreted as teaching this same doctrine in the eighteenth century. It seemed to add up.

I realized then that if maintenance consumption were recovered in pay and products, human depreciation could not also be. There would be nothing left for pure consumption except Mill's "unproductive consumption" neither replacing nor maintaining human capital. That would stand biology on its head. Biology is about replacing and maintaining us. Unproductive consumption, for which there seem to be parallels in other species, is something biology has yet to justify. It cannot be the *unique* taste satisfaction that behavior reveals.

I found a solution that seemed to make sense then. It was the exact opposite of what I think now. If maintenance consumption were recovered in pay and work products, as I now think human depreciation but not maintenance consumption is, then human depreciation instead of maintenance consumption could be exhausted in taste satisfaction! That seemed less macabre to me then. I looked for ways in which human depreciation, the polar opposite of the biological end in itself, could somehow be its measure. Aging, after all, means survival. The old gag says that it is not so bad when you think about the alternative. Age-wage profiles could be explained, I thought then, as recovery of maintenance consumption rather than of human depreciation in pay. And I had those precedents from the eighteenth century. Mill too could be interpreted that way, in his definition of "productive consumption," as could Piero Sraffa in a paper from 1960. I thought I was on the right track.

THE BOSS AND HER SECRETARY

What brought me to my senses was the thought experiment about a boss and her secretary I mentioned earlier. The boss has earned ten times as much throughout their careers. If their pay recovered maintenance consumption as well as realized work, then they would have to hold their maintenance consumption to the same 10:1 ratio, or somehow make up the difference in the timing of their realized work. They probably couldn't do this even if they tried.

I don't claim that this *reductio ad absurdum* meets the standard of logical certainty. So I beef it up with another argument which also seems persuasive without foreclosing debate. My six months and later weekends in the Quartermaster Corps taught me that human needs are fairly uniform. Not that they are entirely so. The general and the boss need more privacy than the GI or secretary, in space to themselves, because their jobs are to plan and think. Higher rank, in the firm or the military, does seem to call for more maintenance consumption overall. But the *range* in consumption needs, from a quartermaster's perspective, seems small in proportion to the range in pay. The general and the GI eat the same chow in the field, and pretty much the same in garrison as well.

That's how I came to the pay rule. We see why it ought to startle economists. Macro teaches that wage measures work, and teaches it so confidently that it uses the notation W for either. That means what I call "realized" work in exchange for literal or imputed pay, as economists know from Schultz and Mincer and others that some work is self-invested. I call this teaching the W doctrine. It misses the recovery rule. All economists, as far as I know, treat human depreciation as deadweight loss. Pay recovers and measures gross realized work, meaning gross of human depreciation, just as gross realized profit recovers physical depreciation. That's why I use "pay" in place of the more usual but baggage-laden "wage."

But the pay rule as a whole is not certainty. I cannot reason from definitions, or even from the causality and convergence axioms, that Quesnay was wrong. If he was right after all, as I understand him, then maintenance consumption would be recovered alongside human depreciation. My current view that it is not can be called the "maintenance exhaust" principle. The pay rule rests on the certainty of expected depreciation recovery and on the common sense, less than certainty, of maintenance exhaust.

QUESNAY'S IDEA

What Quesnay wrote, in his entry for "man" in Diderot's *Encyclopedia* of 1750, was

> "Those who make manufactured commodities do not produce wealth ... they spend their receipts in order to obtain their subsistence. Thus they consume as much as they produce ... and no surplus of wealth results from it."

Mill's *Essays*[2] includes

> "... as much as is necessary to keep the productive worker in perfect health and fitness for his employment, may be said to be consumed productivity. To this should be added what he expends in rearing children to the age at which they become capable of productive industry."

Mill's *Principles* of 1848, which I quoted earlier, said the same:

> "What they consume in keeping up their health, strength and capacities of work, or in rearing the productive laborers to succeed them, is productive consumption."

Sraffa's parallel idea is expressed in his 1960 paper *Production of Commodities by Means of Commodities.*

My impression is that Quesnay's "surplus of wealth" (*produit net*) means value added, and that he thought maintenance consumption should be deducted from revenue in finding it. It seemed to me that Mill and Sraffa might have reasoned partway there.

My belief then that human depreciation is exhausted in satisfying tastes seemed defensible then. I argued, sensibly to a point, that getting older meant surviving. I suppose I might still argue the same but for the parable of the boss and her secretary.

---

2   *Essays on Some Unsettled Questions of Political Economy* (1944).

THE SLAVE PARADOX

Say that Phil enslaves Bill. Bill's maintenance consumption had been taste-satisfying pure consumption to Bill when Bill was free, and so was not deducted from his pay to find his cash flow and output as valued by himself. But Bill's maintenance consumption satisfies no tastes of Phil. Bill's cash flow and output to Phil are both less than they were to himself by the amount of Bill's maintenance. So then, on Phil's books, is Bill's present value of that cash flow.

This *noir* thought experiment is worth thinking through. It shows that even if slavery were legal and common, its market evidence would neither show the value of human capital nor refute the fact that human capital is inalienable. It is inalienable for the reason, if none other, that our maintenance consumption satisfies no one else's tastes. Phil did not acquire Bill's human capital. He converted it to livestock worth much less to him than what it had been as human capital to Bill.

Another useful point is that assets in general tend to be worth more to their owners. This does not contradict the convergence axioms. We buy or build to taste. That difference is particularly important as to assets not meant to be traded, such as productive plant. I suspect that this is what the national accounts missed in adjusting depreciation.

A TWELFTH COMMANDMENT

My favorite among the many proposals for the eleventh commandment is "Thou shall not quit." I forget the source.

My choice for twelfth is "Thou shalt not duck the question." There are exceptions to both, as there are to the first ten, but we know what they mean. I chide human capital economists who have reasoned in terms of human depreciation over half a century for ducking the question of where this huge flow goes.

Not all questions left open are ducked. A book or paper moves the horizon only so far. Answering one question means posing another. Ducking one means leaving an obvious one unasked. It means leaving the elephant in the room or skeleton in the closet out of the report. Human depreciation itself has been noticed and mentioned everywhere, since Schultz, as the negative component in human growth. Somebody, somewhere, should have asked out loud where that investment ends up in an accounting sense. A good auditor follows the money through. I personally interpret Ben-Porath and tradition as evanescing it away in deadweight loss, six feet under, for new output to replenish. But other readings may be possible. Somehow it was left to this amateur to pose the question out loud and suggest a different answer.

Refuting a Piketty Argument

There are practical uses for the pay rule aside from solution of the age-wage problem. These give the pay rule's impact on tax laws and public policy that I promised. Piketty, in papers and in his bestselling book, follows arguments I don't accept to conclusions I do in part. Although his main argument is put another way, the gist is that the ratio of pay to net profit rose substantially during the world wars, world depression and welfare state period following, and has declined since. His evidence is what I call the "Piketty U-curve"; physical capital and net profit fell in ratio to other values including pay, consumption and net national product over that period, in many countries, and have since recovered. Piketty is right so far. He argues for higher inheritance and capital taxes in consequence. His argument follows tradition in comparing pay and net profit as the shares of workers and investors in income.

But tradition is wrong. Pay is the worker's gross realized income, meaning gross of human depreciation. Depreciation, for either factor, is a steadier flow. This makes gross output for either less responsive to upturns and downturns. It is a particularly high share of realized income or output in hard times when dislocation of both factors (human and physical capital) drives net output of each down. Comparison between net income and gross realized income can mislead. I happen to share Piketty's enthusiasm for stiff inheritance taxes, though gosh knows where I would be if I hadn't inherited wealth. But I don't think the case for them needs unsound arguments.

Piketty's argument is complex, and will get a more direct and thorough treatment in the section in mathematical notation at the end of my final chapter.

Connecting the Pay and Output Rules

It happens that capital growth and output are examples of "additive" variables; the sum of growths and outputs of the parts gives the growth or output of the whole. So then is their difference in cash flow. Some common economic variables are not. Quesnay showed famously that if we add the prices of wheat and flour and bread, as happens when we add the revenues of the wheat farm and flour mill and bakery, we count the price of wheat three times and of flour twice.

Positive cash flow in general is the flow available for reinvestment in other assets including human capital of the same owner, or for gift to others, or for pure consumption. Negative cash flow is the same as gift received. If "net gift" means gift given out less gift received in, then cash flow at the scale of total capital of an individual comes to net gift plus pure consumption. Cash flow of human capital, at that or any scale, was reasoned with less than certainty to equal pay less invested consumption. Algebra shows that net gift plus pure consumption less pay plus invested consumption (two negatives make a positive) gives consumption plus net gift less pay if those two kinds of consumption are the only ones. That too is less than certain for the same reason: I cannot prove that Quesnay and my old view were wrong. If I am right now, algebra shows

individual cash flow = net gift + pure consumption
= human cash flow + physical cash flow

$$= \text{pay} - \text{invested consumption}$$
$$+ \text{physical cash flow,}$$

from which we get the "physical cash flow rule"

$$\text{physical cash flow} = \text{net gift} + \text{pure consumption}$$
$$- \text{pay} + \text{invested consumption}$$
$$= \text{consumption} - \text{pay} + \text{net gift,}$$

given that pure plus invested consumption sum to all consumption. At the collective scale, where net gift cancels out, this simplifies to

$$\text{physical cash flow} = \text{consumption} - \text{pay.}$$

Profit, the output of physical capital, is revealed by the total return truism as growth plus cash flow of physical capital. This and the physical cash flow rule give profit as investment (growth in physical capital) plus consumption less pay at the collective scale. This time the math is

$$\text{profit} = \text{investment} + \text{physical cash flow}$$
$$= \text{investment} + \text{consumption} - \text{pay}$$
$$= \text{investment} + \text{consumption} - \text{realized work}$$
$$- \text{human depreciation,}$$

at the collective scale. Now the output rule

output = investment + consumption
+ self-invested work – human depreciation,

with the facts

output = work + profit   and
work = self-invested work + realized work

reveal the output and pay rules as mutually implicit.

What I have tried to do here is to show how those two fit together through the nexus of the physical cash flow rule. That rule will prove useful through its exceptional tractability; consumption and pay are among the most reliably measured quantities in national accounts, and can probably be made more so. Profit then becomes directly measurable as the sum of physical cash flow and growth in market-valued capital.

SUMMARY AND DISCUSSION

That gives the outline. It is a layman's view of what a proper economist might not have attempted. Fools rush in. I will continue to cite sources in economics and biology not to pretend that I am an authority, but to give real ones a chance to check.

The main surprises I promised, aside from free growth itself, are the pay and output rules and next generation theory. My depreciation theory is a surprise too, particularly because it reverses traditional doctrine 180 degrees. Value loss is almost nothing at the start, and essentially all of cash flow at the end. I include depreciation theory on that ground, but more because it rounds out the pay rule and so helps explain age-wage profiles. My risk theory—unusual in that it infers the riskiness of the asset from the risk profile of the owner rather than conversely—completes the explanation. We modify our human as much as our physical capital to current risk tolerance. Our portfolio compositions decline in risk and return as we age. This refutes any hypothesis that age-wage profiles reflect rising productivity of human capital as distinct from recovery of its depreciation. Pay at the end is all human depreciation and no realized work.

What makes my book different, aside from my lack of credentials, is the surprises and the unusual degree of abstraction leading to them. Not many writers try to follow a chain of inference as far without the comforting touch of the stone and wood and rope. If Becker had been as venturesome, he might well have solved the age-wage problem in 1964. I see no other path. Economics is all inside. It is tastes expressed in choices. Capital is foreseen satisfactions discounted by whatever our taste for impatience is. Most of it is human capital leaving little market record beyond its rental cost in pay. Logic is left with much of the burden.

There is no escaping the recovery rule. The deadweight loss rule is unanswerable. The maximand rule is unanswerable. The last-day paradox is unanswerable. Age-wage profiles have no other explanation consistent with the definition of human capital as present value. These profiles are illustration of the recovery rule, rather than proof, because logical certainty is proved only by analysis. Empirical tests show only that a given result is possible. A hundred repetitions prove it possible a hundred times. Certainties are certain always.

Predictions of behavior can work because tastes converge to market equilibria. What stands behind the convergence, I argue, is biology selecting tastes that maintain and reproduce us. The idea that we act out the biological imperative is clear in Petty and Malthus, and in the equilibrium wage theory of Adam Smith and David Ricardo, where pay converges to the level preserving the work force. But if I say everything about that now, I will have nothing to say later.

NOTATION

DEPRECIATION THEORY

The round trip truism can show as $\delta = r_m$, where δ and r_m are time-preference rate and rate of return to market as before. Unsubscripted r, in these equations, will mean r_m. Let "value" V mean any mix of human capital H and physical capital K. They sum to total capital $K_T = H+K$. Then V and K_T mean the same. The present value rule is

$$V(0) = \int_0^\infty F(t)e^{-r(t)t} \, dt \, , \qquad (3.1)$$

where t=0 gives present time and t gives future time. F(t) gives cash flow (value withdrawn less value concurrently invested from outside) expected at future time t.

Our taste for reliability and predictability tends to demand assets of steady performance or "utility" until replaced, and utility tends to be measured in cash flow. Meanwhile there seems to be no clear reason to suppose that time preference rate r is a function of asset age except for human capital. Then let F and r be taken as constant. For assets of finite lifespan ω, if so, value at asset age x is

$$V(x) = F \int_x^{\omega} e^{-r(t-x)} dt = \frac{F}{r}\left[1 - e^{-r(\omega-x)}\right], \quad \text{giving} \tag{3.2}$$

$$V'(x) = -Fe^{-r(\omega-x)} = -Fe^{-r\omega}e^{rx}, \quad r\omega \geq 1. \tag{3.3}$$

The condition $r\omega \geq 1$ is required because value decline $-\dot{V}'(x)$ would otherwise exceed cash flow F to leave an unrecovered residue of deadweight loss. Given $r\omega \geq 1$, (3.3) shows that value decline begins at a minimum and increases exponentially, contradicting general belief.

Further understanding comes with evaluation of aggregates over asset lifespan ω. Aggregate output, by (3.2) and the definition $r = V/Y$, is

$$\int_0^{\omega} Y(x)dt = r\int_0^{\omega} V(x)dt = F\int_0^{\omega}\left[1 - e^{-r\omega}e^{rx}\right]dx = F\omega - Fe^{-r\omega}\int_0^{\omega} e^{rx}dx$$

$$= F\left[\omega - e^{-r\omega}\frac{e^{r\omega}-1}{r}\right] = \frac{F}{r}\left[r\omega + e^{-r\omega} - 1\right].$$

Then aggregate flow $F\omega$ exceeds aggregate output by the difference

$$F\omega - \frac{F}{r}\left[r\omega + e^{-r\omega} - 1\right] = \frac{F}{r}\left[1 - e^{r\omega}\right].$$

Meanwhile V(0), the capital value from which decline begins, is also

$$V(0) = \frac{F}{r}\left[1 - e^{-r\omega}\right],$$

again by (3.2). This confirms that aggregate cash flow is exactly enough to capture aggregate output together with depreciation of all original capital V(0).

This reasoning from aggregates was not strictly necessary. Recovery of all output in cash flow was already implied in the choice of r as the discount rate. What is shown here is the mechanism. It is worth adding to the argument because (3.3) contradicts tradition diametrically, and settled opinion dies hard.

It needn't follow that depreciation in itself grows exponentially, because self-invested output or plowback from gross realized output contribute a positive growth component which depreciation must overcome to maintain that overall trajectory. This study will leave those components unpredicted individually. Their net effect, under assumptions, is shown in (3.3).

The assumptions of constant F and r do not apply to human capital, where pay rises deep into careers while risk aversion and implicitly time-preference rate should tend to decline per risk theory. It seems plausible to treat each input of self-invested work and adult invested consumption accounting for the rise in pay as adding separate new skills to be applied constantly, and each to yield a separate stream of constant utility and cash flow from separate starting points until all human capital and human cash flow end together. An individual's overall human capital would then compare to a collection of investments each meeting the criterion of constant F, although not of constant r, required to arrive at (3.3).

THE PHYSICAL CASH FLOW RULE

(2.6) shows cash flow at the individual scale as net gift γ plus pure consumption C_p. Human cash flow at any scale was derived as pay π less invested consumption C_s. By additivity of cash flow, physical cash flow F_K at the individual scale is

$$F_K = \gamma + C_p - (\pi - C_s) = \gamma + C_p - \pi + C_s = C + \gamma - \pi. \qquad (3.4)$$

At the collective scale, where gift cancels out, this reduces to

$$F_K = C - \pi . \qquad (3.5)$$

Profit P, meanwhile, is the output of physical capital. By the total return truism, output is growth plus cash flow. This and (3.4) show

$$P = \dot{K} + F = \dot{K} + C - \pi$$

at the collective scale. Arrange as

$$\dot{K} + C = P + \pi. \qquad (3.6)$$

Then if investment I is understood as growth in physical capital $\dot{K}$, this can also be written as

$$I + C = P + \pi, \tag{3.6a}$$

showing that the traditional beliefs $Y = I + C$ and $Y = P + \pi$ are mutually consistent.

The reason for this consistency is found in the pay rule $\pi = W_p + D_H = W - W_s + D_H$ True output is the sum of factor outputs $Y = W + P = \pi + P + W_s - D_H$. This is why the Y and W doctrines each miss self-invested work W_s but mistakenly include human depreciation D_H.

4

HUMAN CAPITAL ACCOUNTING

How Many Factors?

Why split all value into two factors only? Why not acknowledge social or cultural capital, as when a symphony orchestra comes to more than the sum of its parts? Aren't science and tradition and rule of law kinds of capital too?

They are. But the question posed was whether treating them as fundamental kinds, joining or replacing physical and human capital, could shorten the path to understanding and explaining. That invites a review of what has seemed fundamental so far.

Most classical economists from Petty in the seventeenth century through Mill in the nineteenth accepted three factors in land, labor and manufactures. Their owners, meaning landlords, workers and investors, were seen as forming three separate and politically competing classes. Indeed they were for millennia. As agriculture gradually ceded its dominance, the distinction between land and manu-factures seemed less to warrant separate factors. Over the last century or so, "capital" has tended to include land in a two-factor system of capital and labor. Some followed Mill's contemporaries John Rae and Nassau Senior in interpreting capital as labor compounded over the period of production, so that the prime factors were time and labor. Many since Schultz and Mincer a half century ago, including me, prefer to put the two as physical and human capital. Meanwhile the idea of separate classes owning those factors has found less usefulness. All people are workers, and all adults are property investors too.

Many of the classicists, from Quesnay and Adam Smith through Mill, distinguished capital and labor and consump-tion into productive and unproductive components. The marginalists, who showed how supply, demand and price come together at a point called the margin, tended to dispute this dichotomy as unscientific and judgmental. We apply resources to satisfy tastes, whether for gain or leisure or mischief. I too make no such distinction. Thus I follow Irving Fisher in including consumer goods and belongings of every kind, including land, in physical capital. All are covertly productive. Even cash in our pockets yields psychic return in the comfort of liquidity. Whatever has a value to us can influence our choices and counts as capital.

How and why do I distinguish the two factors? Human capital is the factor whose maintenance cost, meaning maintenance consumption, satisfies the worker's taste for survival and so is not deducted from revenue, meaning pay, in calculating her subjective cash flow and output. The slave paradox showed that the inalienability of human capital follows from this root difference. I showed how I once believed something else, following Quesnay, and how a thought experiment about a boss and her secretary set me right.

These two factors, human and physical, are enough for my purposes. I see them as enough to accommodate a range of configurations in social or cultural capital, much as complex structures can be described in terms of time, space and mass. Analysis from basic elements is not inherently reductionist. It is what we have to do if we want to understand.

But there is also truth behind the cultural capital idea. It is the essence of institutionalism or historicism. Economics needs this analysis, particularly in explaining why some societies and not others participate in growth. What I don't see is a gain in treating culture as a prime factor. It is a way in which the two prime ones are organized.

SHOULD ECONOMICS TAKE CUES FROM PHYSICS?

"Why can't a woman," gripes Henry Higgins, "be more like a man?" We all know that the answer is *vive la difference.* Economics can envy the success of physics, but must find its own way.

One difference is that physics reasons upward from data, in the main, while economics usually reasons downward from assumptions or axioms. Physics finds reliable patterns, and terms them laws of nature until the pattern fails. Why are Planck's or Boltzmann's or the gravitational constant what they seem to be, or the magnetic permeability of space, instead of other numbers just as plausible? Ours not to reason why. But ours to keep on measuring in case the next sample reveals an exception.

Economic axioms have tended to trust what logically ought to be true, and seems true enough in experience. We begin with a notion of oughtness along with waiting for patterns to reveal themselves. There is a sense of *why* behind the perceptions of how and what. This deductive or *a priori* method has proved the general rule in economic thought from the classicists through the present. We infer from axiom or hypothesis, and check conclusions against the data only at the end.

Some campaign for the opposite. Historicists and institutionalists have claimed more kinship with the inductive or *a posteriori* method that has marked the triumph of physics. Gosh knows, economics could use such a triumph. And it needs more input from historicists and institutionalists. More power to them.

But *vive la difference.* My personal way, although not all the time, is the old-fashioned *a priori* one. These ideas in this book generally seemed obvious from the inside. When I gathered that they didn't seem so to others, I began to think up ways to test them.

Underlying all these reasons for a deductive approach is the opacity of the larger factor. Human capital, I and many others have noted, leaves little market record apart from its rental cost in pay. Let's see what more can be found about it.

HISTORY OF THE HUMAN CAPITAL IDEA

The term human capital is touchy because it can suggest that life has a price. Irving Fisher used it in quotation marks in 1898,[1] attributing it to earlier sources I haven't found, but not in his two great books on the topic in 1906[2] and 1907.[3]

The concept began with Petty in 1664.[4] He estimated the aggregate pay of English workers, and divided by the discount rate he had modeled in *A Treatise of Taxes* two years earlier. I have not read *Verbum Sapienti* (a word to the wise), but have read two of his later versions of the same argument.[5]

Petty's method was criticized by William Farr in 1854,[6] also in a paper I haven't read, for neglecting what I call invested consumption. Farr, if I read the right description of his argument, was correct in principle. Human capital is present value of pay less invested consumption. Petty took no account of the latter. But it would be a mistake to conclude as Farr did that Petty overestimated the value of human capital. I will argue in the next chapter that by underestimating the generation length in *A Treatise of*

---

[1] *The Nature of Capital.*
[2] *The Nature of Capital and Income.*
[3] *The Rate of Interest.*
[4] *Verbum Sapienti.*
[5] *Political Arithmetic* (1676) and *A Gross Estimate of the Wealth of England* (1685).
[6] *Vital Statistics.*

Taxes, Petty applied too steep a discount rate. Meanwhile he had to invent his own national accounts from which to measure aggregate pay. He measured human capital as only about 1.5 times physical capital. Modern measures find 2 to 4 times, or even more.

Keynes' teacher Alfred Marshall effectively agreed with Farr in 1990.[7] As I read his passage, Marshall interpreted maintenance consumption supporting present pay as investment adding future pay. So did B. F. Kiker[8] in 1968, if I read him right. All three men, I think, were right in deducting invested consumption from pay to find what I call human cash flow, but wrong in deducting maintenance consumption as well.

Meanwhile economists had developed the complementary idea of human capital as present cost of investment already accumulated. Smith[9] in 1776 wrote

> ... The acquisition of such talents, by the maintenance of the acquirer during his education, study, or apprenticeship, always costs a real expense, which is a capital fixed and realized, as it were, in his person.

Mincer seems to have been first in print with the post-war revival of interest in human capital, in his 1958 paper[10] rederiving Fisher's present value equation and stressing job training. Schultz impresses me as the main

---

[7] *Principles of Economics.*
[8] *A History of Human Capital.* I learned of Farr from Kiker.
[9] *The Wealth of Nations.*
[10] *Investment in Human Capital and Personal Income Distribution.*

idea man among these post-war contributors. He usually avoided math, unlike the others, and is probably the best source for quotes in plain English. His paper *Investment in Human Capital*, published in 1961, includes:

> ... Much of what we call consumption constitutes investment in human capital. Direct expenditures on education, health and internal migration to take advantage of better job opportunities are clear examples. Earnings foregone by mature students attending school and by workers acquiring on-the-job training are equally clear examples.

> ... This use of leisure time to improve skills and knowledge is widespread ... I shall contend that such investment in human capital accounts for most of the impressive rise in the real earnings per worker ...

> ... Measured by what labor contributes to output, the productive capacity of human beings is now vastly larger than all other forms of wealth taken together ...

> ... the curve relating income to age tends to be steeper for skilled than for unskilled persons. Investment in on-the-job training seems a likely explanation...

> ... We can think of three classes of expenditures: expenditures that satisfy human preferences and in no way enhance the capabilities under discussion – these represent pure consumption; expenditures that enhance capabilities and do not satisfy any preference

underlying consumption – these represent pure investment; and expenditures that ... are ... partly consumption and partly investment, ...

In 1962[11] he added:

... the investment in human capital can conveniently
be classified in (1) nurture and higher education, (2)
postschool training and learning, (3) preschool learning activities, (4) migration, (5) health, (6) information,
and (7) investment in children (population) ...

... But unlike the wonderful "one-hoss shay," the productive life of educational capital typically does not
go to pieces all at once. It depreciates along the way, it
becomes obsolete, it is altered by changes in retirement
and by the state of employment ...

... As already noted, educational capital, like reproduc-
ible physical capital, is subject to depreciation and obsolescence. The established tax treatment takes account
of both depreciation and obsolescence in the case of
physical capital, but this accounting is not extended to
education capital... In brief, our tax laws ... appear to be
all but blind to the fact that educational capital entails
maintenance and depreciation, becomes obsolete, and
disappears at death...

These excerpts clearly show Shultz's meanings of pure
and invested consumption, and of human deprecation. We

---

[11] *Human Capital: Policy Issues and Research Opportunities.*

also see his belief, with which I disagree, that substantial invested consumption continues after independence and physical maturity. For example, he writes "Direct expenditures on ... health and internal migration ... are clear examples." I interpret these outlays, when applied to adult workers, as maintenance consumption preserving rather than adding skills, and enabling current pay rather than invested for higher pay later. Even some adult schooling, I believe, is designed to update existing skills and so preserve current pay rather than to create new skills and higher pay. I call this "maintenance schooling."

I agree that self-invested work "to improve skills and knowledge ... accounts for most of the impressive rise in the real earnings per worker ..." But I don't share Schultz's view that the "use of leisure time" accounts for much of this improvement. My years in plants and oilfields and offices have given me an impression of some study by workers during leisure time, but mostly passive accumulation of experience and insight while fully at work on the job.

I showed why I don't agree that human depreciation, or any depreciation, need imply any obsolescence or erosion en route to the inevitable date with the wrecking ball or St. Peter. Rather we depreciate for the reason that makes mortgages amortize. Even as we earn more and more, more and more of our earning days are behind us. Sooner or later, long after retirement, comes the last day. Human capital becomes present value of one day's imputed pay, less one day's discount at the time preference rate visible in our security accounts, even if our pay and performance have reached career highs. As long as we know the time when the one-hoss shay is expected to go to pieces, we deprecate it gradually to zero at that point just as with ordinary shays.

MAINTENANCE LEARNING

My impression from experience is that most self-invested work is passive job experience costing no down time for study. If I am right, our cost of adult learning was paid in our formative years, when we gathered skills to process experience quickly, and needs little if any supplement now. Thus self-invested work might continue almost to the end, and still recover that slight cost with interest in higher pay later. But pay seems to stabilize some time before retirement. Then so does self-invested work. What continues, I think, is what I call "maintenance learning." It can arrive as the complement of maintenance schooling, or as observation on our own. It is defined as learning to keep up pay now rather than to enhance pay later. At all ages, we must learn the names and traits of new clients and co-workers and suppliers continually, along with new constraints and opportunities in the world outside, in order to do what we are already paid for. Maintenance learning is realized work recovered in pay and work product now, not self-invested work for pay enhancement later.

DID THE MARGINALISTS RECOGNIZE HUMAN CAPITAL?

The marginalist tradition, which has dominated economic thought since its introduction by William Stanley Jevons and Carl Menger in 1871, has treated all consumption as the end point exhausting capital in satisfying tastes. It doesn't follow that marginalists were unaware that some is invested in human capital. At least three of the leading ones understood human capital well. That includes Leon Walras, a later co-founder of the marginalist revolution in 1874. I already mentioned Marshall and Irving Fisher. But all three, and marginalists in general, preferred to locate human capital outside the economy proper. Whether they spoke of labor measured in dollars per unit time, or human capital measured in dollars alone, the larger factor was taken to arrive exogenously. It provided its services from outside and was paid their market value in return, as if on the books of a firm, which likewise hires workers without owning them or accounting for their sources.

HUMAN CAPITAL AND THE VALUE-ADDED CHAIN

Value added is another term for (net) output or total return or creation of value. The value-added chain is a concept we owe to Quesnay and the physiocrats. Wheat, in their favorite example, is incorporated into flour and flour into bread. Quesnay pointed out that we can't add the prices of products and their components without duplication. The thing to count at each stage was value added, or price realized less price paid to the stage or stages before.

The human capital concept, particularly in description of the roles of invested consumption and self-invested work and human depreciation by Mincer and Schultz and Ben-Porath, has begun the endogenization or inclusion of human capital within the chain. The pay rule furthers that process by accounting for the disposition of human capital. It is recovered within the chain in revenue and cash flow, just as with depreciation of the wheat farm and mill and bakery.

WHEN DOES HUMAN CAPITAL END?

Retirement generally means the period or first moment when people end the careers for which their training has been specialized. The reason is typically not diminished skills and performance just yet, as age-wage profiles show no little or no drop in pay toward the end. I think it is more that we and our bosses see the drop coming.

Literal pay is typically zero in retirement. Instead we earn imputed pay for taking care of ourselves and one another, and for driving the grandkids to the zoo. These services are tangible, not psychic, in that they save the hire of others to do the same. The imputed pay is what the others would have charged. But it typically is not enough to meet our consumption needs. Retirees must typically draw down savings or depend on "social transfer payments," meaning support from government or family or institutions, to make ends meet.

These infusions from savings or transfer cannot be invested consumption to be recovered with interest in higher pay later. There will be no later. And the imputed pay of retirees figures to decline with age, rather than to rise. Their transfer received is spent on pure consumption recovered now in the satisfaction of survival. Then human cash flow, or pay less invested consumption, remains positive to the end if we recognize imputed pay and treat invested consumption by elders as nil. It follows that human capital, as present value of human cash flow, continues to the end as well.

COMPLETING THE BEN-PORATH MODEL

Ben-Porath's 1967 paper, translating his terms to mine, sees all consumption and all work as self-invested until independence at maturity. Realized work and human depreciation are modeled to begin at that age. A progressively smaller share of work and/or consumption continues to be self-invested until late in careers so as to explain age-wage profiles. Human capital increases as long as these two together exceed human depreciation, and declines toward zero as their sum becomes progressively less. My analysis agrees on all these points. I would complement his model by applying the pay rule and my depreciation theory. Ben-Porath's equation explaining pay is most easily read as implying that pay equals realized work alone. It should be adjusted to show the pay rule, and to show that the share of recovered human depreciation rises to all of pay at the end.

HUMAN CAPITAL AND THE FIRM

Pay, literal or imputed, can be interpreted as the revenue of human capital. It is analogous to revenue of a firm. The firm's revenue goes first to pay what I call "prior claims" for outside contributions by workers and suppliers. The counterpart to these outside costs for human capital would be maintenance consumption enabling pay. I said how I thought for years that this should be deducted as a claim on pay, just as with the firm, and how the parable of the boss and secretary set me straight. What I think now is more in line with what economists have taught me since the marginalist revolution a century and half ago: maintenance is exhausted in satisfying our taste for personal and lineage survival. It is recovered in that satisfaction alone, and not in transfer to product value. I call this the maintenance exhaust principle. It implies

prior claims on pay = nil.

The firm's revenue less prior claims leaves gross realized output, meaning realized (sold) output plus depreciation. As human capital does not deduct its parallel cost of maintenance consumption, its gross realized output (gross realized work) is the same as its revenue in pay. The logic is

$$\text{gross realized work} = \text{pay} - \text{prior claims on pay}$$
$$= \text{pay}.$$

The firm then subtracts depreciation from gross realized output to leave realized output. The pay rule shows that accounting for human capital follows the same logic. Thus

$$\text{realized work} = \text{gross realized work} - \text{human depreciation}$$
$$= \text{pay} - \text{human depreciation},$$

showing the pay rule.

The firm may also produce "proprietary output" not yet sold or not meant to be sold. Examples include output to inventory, or capital construction as when a contractor builds its own offices or when an automaker makes cars for its executive fleet. Output is the sum of these realized and proprietary components. The proprietary and realized output of human capital are self-invested and realized work, which sum to all of work as proprietary and realized output sum to output in the firm. That shows as

$$\text{self-invested work} + \text{realized work} = \text{work}.$$

The treatment of cash flow is also parallel. Positive cash flow from the firm to investors is dividend yield, or gross realized output less plowback. The analogy for human capital is

$$\text{positive human cash flow} = \text{pay} - \text{pay plowback},$$

where the last term includes tuition and textbooks bought from pay.

Negative cash flow to the firm is outside investment raised in new stock issues. All outside investment in human capital, in a broader sense including pay plowback, is summed up as invested consumption. "Outside" here doesn't necessarily mean from outsiders. The source of invested consumption might be parental gift, or the worker's pay, or cash in her bank account or food in her refrigerator. The definition is

$$\text{invested consumption} = \text{negative human cash flow} + \text{pay plowback,}$$

which can be arranged as

$$\text{negative human cash flow} = \text{invested consumption} - \text{pay plowback.}$$

Now we find the human cash flow rule

$$\begin{aligned}\text{human cash flow} &= \text{positive human cash flow} \\ &\quad - \text{negative human cash flow} \\ &= \text{pay} - \text{invested consumption.}\end{aligned}$$

Growth too follows the same accounting logic in human capital as in the firm. It begins with negative cash flow, meaning new investment from outside. For the firm, that means investment raised from new share issues. Proprietary or self-invested output adds more growth. The remaining positive component is plowback from revenue, and the negative one is depreciation. Then for the firm,

> growth = negative cash flow
> > \+ self-invested (or proprietary) output
> > \+ plowback from revenue
> > – recovered depreciation.

I call this reasoning from elimination of alternatives the "growth truism."

Human capital growth follows the same logic. Self-invested work, pay plowback and human depreciation become the counterparts to proprietary output, plowback from revenue and recovered decapitalization. Then

> human growth = negative human cash flow
> > \+ self-invested work + pay plowback
> > – human depreciation.

Now the definition

> invested consumption = negative human cash flow
> > \+ pay plowback

allows

> human growth = invested consumption
> > \+ self-invested work – human depreciation,

confirming the Ben-Porath equation.

THE ACCOUNTINGS COMPARED SIDE BY SIDE

Accounting treatments of the firm and human capital, substituting "profit" for "output" in the firm, can be compared as follows:

Category	Firm	Human Capital
Revenue:	Proceeds from sales.	Pay.
Prerequisite for sales:	Labor, supplies etc.	Maintenance consumption.
Prior claims:	Same as above.	None.
Gross realized output:	Gross realized profit; revenue less prior claims.	Gross realized work, equivalently pay.
Plowback:	Reinvestment of earned revenue within the firm.	Pay plowback; reinvestment of pay in the earner's own human capital.
Positive cash flow:	Dividend yield; gross realized profit less plowback.	Pay less pay plowback.
Negative cash flow:	Capital raised in new stock issues.	Invested consumption less pay plowback.
Cash flow:	Dividend yield less new stock issues.	Pay less invested consumption
Realized output:	Gross realized profit less depreciation.	Pay less human depreciation.

Unrealized output:	Proprietary profit.	Self-invested work.
Output:	Profit; realized plus unrealized profit.	Work; re-alized plus self-invested work.
Growth:	New capital raised plus unre-alized profit plus plowback less recovered depre-ciation.	Invested con-sumption plus self-invested work less human depre-ciation.

ACCOUNTING FOR THE INDIVIDUAL

Human cash flow above was specified as pay less invested consumption by the human cash flow rule, while cash flow of the firm was not specified by the physical cash flow rule. Both rules describe at the scale of the total capital of the individual owner. Their variables are pay, invested consumption, consumption as a whole, pay, and net gift. Each is a property of the owner of capital rather than of capital in itself. Human capital and its human owner are coextensive and inseparable, although not identical, while shares in the firm trade among many owners who may each trade in shares of other firms as well. The physical cash flow rule applies to all shares together owned by an individual at a given moment, along with all other property claims.

This book puts a special focus on the economics of the biological individual, at every age, as distinct from the economics of the household or nation. The last day paradox and owner rule, as well as both the human and physical cash flow rules, are cases in point. This theme will continue in the next chapter.

SUMMARY

What Schultz, Mincer, Becker, Ben-Porath and other human capital economists began a half century ago was the inclusion or endogenization of human capital as a product within the value-added chain. Wheat, flour, bread, human capital. The pay rule continues the endogenization by spelling out where human depreciation goes. Endogenization makes the economy like a single all-inclusive firm. We ourselves stand outside, as with stockholders in any firm, but our human capital begins and ends inside. Think of us as tastes without means, and of our human capital as means without tastes. Our human capital interprets our tastes, and manages both factors to meet them.

Something in us resents this endogenization as impudent and demeaning. Not so. Remember that human capital doesn't mean us. It means the value of our skills, not our souls, to ourselves and no one else. We rent them out for pay, and take no offense when the market bids so much and no more for them. We realize that when we work on our own projects, they are worth so much and no more to ourselves. We pay so much and no more for them when we earn our way through college. That makes their present value, to us alone, whatever we expect them to earn over the future less whatever we discount for delay.

Human capital accounting is broadly analogous to accounting in a firm. The revenue of human capital is pay. I follow business accounting practice in distinguishing maintenance from investment; invested consumption is expected to be recovered with interest in higher pay later, while maintenance, as in the firm, fulfills a condition on which that expectation was premised. But our maintenance is not deducted from our revenue to leave our gross realized output, as with the firm, if we accept the maintenance exhaust principle. Thus pay and gross realized work become the same. Realized work is that less recovered human depreciation, and work is this difference plus unrealized work.

The growth equations for the firm and human capital are also parallel. Growth of each is investment from outside plus self-invested output plus plowback from revenue less depreciation. For human capital, this simplifies to invested consumption plus self-invested work less human depreciation.

What Farr, Marshall and Kiker have shown, by deducting both invested and maintenance consumption from pay to get adult cash flow discounted to present value, is human livestock value to a slave owner. It is very little. The slave paradox argued that the slave's maintenance is expensed on the slave owner's books, but treated as net output and positive cash flow on the slave's.

5

NEXT GENERATION THEORY

OUTLINE OF THE ARGUMENT

My topic here is time-preference rate. The argument combines an insight of Petty in 1662 with the period of production theory first proposed by the Scotsman John Rae in 1834. Petty realized that time-preference rate explains rate of return; we will wait only so long to recover our investment in cash flow. What we really produce is the next generation, and the age gap between generations gives the time it takes. He reckoned the gap, now called the generation length, at 21 years. Rate of return or time-preference would equal the reciprocal of that period, meaning one over it. That comes to about 4.8% per year.

Period of production theory reasons alike to a point. Production takes so much time, and return or time-preference rate becomes the reciprocal of that period. Faster production, higher returns. The theory never became mainstream because it didn't add much predictive value. It needed only Petty's insight for completion. The next generation is the final product, and its period of production is the generation length.

I amend Petty's idea in two features. He figured the generation length at 21 years by a primogenesis approach. I prefer population geneticist R.A. Fisher's definition equal-weighting all births from first to last. That gives 28.5 years, by my reckoning, so that the reciprocal drops from Petty's 4.8% to 3.5%. And I interpret this as the collective cash flow or pure consumption rate alone, rather than the rate of return as a whole. My reason here is that the reciprocal of the generation length gives the generation *replacement* rate, not the creation rate including growth. Free growth rate is added exogenously to complete the explanation of return.

The generation length is a biological norm which may not have varied much since earliest records. This means that next generation theory can be tested against data from any period. We know that it predicts only at the collective scale. Collective return is average-risk return. Subtract collective growth rate from average-risk return to leave collective cash flow rate. Return and growth are two of the most closely measured rates in economics. Then tests of next generation theory, which predicts their difference, should be practical. I will show evidence in dividend rates since 1700 and interest rates from Sumerian times.

Period of Production Theory

Rae[1] was mentioned as a contributor to what later developed into Mill's free growth theory. Rae's period of production theory in the same book reasoned that production took time, and that profit compensated the investor's patience over the production period. Nassau Senior, who had sent Rae's book to Mill, adopted this idea in his own better-known *Outline*.[2] Rae's book itself found few readers, despite its warm endorsement by Mill in his own *Principles* of 1848. Jevons worked out the math in 1871, and Eugen von Böhm-Bawerk developed the concept from Senior and Jevons in his book of 1889. Böhm-Bawerk soon learned of Rae's work, and dedicated later editions to him. Period of production theory thrives today in the Austrian School, which was founded by Böhm-Bawerk's model Carl Menger in the same year 1871.

It has found little favor elsewhere. The period seemed impractical to define or measure, and so gave little predictive value. Joseph Schumpeter, a student of Böhm-Bawerk who disagreed with him on this point, argued in 1911 that the period of production is zero; capital is present continuously. Frank Knight, who had anticipated Schultz in realizing that some consumption is investment in human capital, argued as Schumpeter had. Irving Fisher, a champion of Böhm Bawerk's beautiful inference that time preference explains rate of return rather than conversely, leaves out his period of production theory.

---

[1]   *New Principals of Political Economy (1834).*
[2]   *An Outline of the Science of Political Economy (1836).*

But the theory is true by definition. Any rate is the inverse or reciprocal of a period. The inverse of 4% per year, for example, is 25 years. Return is the ratio of net output to capital producing it, meaning the rate of production, and its reciprocal is the period of production. Schumpeter and Knight were arguing against the facts of algebra. Where they were right was in finding a lack of clarity and predictive value in the theory. Where does it lead? Rabbits and redwoods have different periods of production, at first glance, but should nonetheless agree in return if in risk. Jevons wrote that he meant production of the "wage fund" as a whole, meaning the universe of consumer goods. Rae, Senior and Böhm-Bawerk seem to have meant the same. But Jevons pointed to wine and timber as examples to help pin down the period. Böhm-Bawerk picked nine years for no reason I can see.

They were on the right track in modeling consumption as the end point of the period. They also realized that the period ending there gives the period of replacement only, and equals the period of production only if capital growth is zero. What they missed was the conversion of some consumption into human capital prolonging the chain, so that only pure consumption marks the end. Then how might we predict the period from creation to pure consumption?

Call that the pure consumption period, for now, so that its reciprocal (inverse) comes to the pure consumption rate. True return is that plus capital growth rate. Rae, Senior, Jevons and Böhm-Bawerk got no farther. But their achievement in modeling the collective pure consumption rate is huge. They missed only human capital. And they could have caught that too. All would also have known of Petty's human and total capital idea, which was occasionally revived and critiqued as by Farr. They didn't quite connect the dots.

NEXT GENERATION THEORY

Petty wrote *A Treatise of Taxes* in 1662. The whole title continues to about as many words, counting ampersands, as pages in the book or pamphlet. Petty dictated his books overnight, munching handfuls of raisins, to secretaries who slept by turns. It is easy to believe that Petty didn't need much sleep. He was a go-getter who had sailed to Ireland as chief medical officer to Cromwell's Ironsides, stayed on to survey the Irish land with which Cromwell would pay his troops, and then got Parliament's approval to invest in that high-risk land to make a fortune.

It is rare for a man of practical gifts to be a deep thinker too. Petty, like my father, was both. His *Verbum Sapienti* of 1664 was first to apply the ancient capitalization formula to both factors, meaning workers as well as tradeable things, and so originated the concept of human capital as present value. Remember that he applied this insight there and in his *Political Arithmetick* in 1676, and again in *The Total Wealth of England* in 1685, to measure the of sum of physical and human capital. That makes him the father of national accounts. But his greatest achievements, I think, came in *A Treatise of Taxes*.

Chapter 4, paragraph 9 of that book begins with

19. Having found the Rent or value of the usus fructus per annum, the question is, how many years purchase (as we usually say) is the Fee simple naturally worth? If we say an infinite number, then an Acre of Land would be equal in value to a thousand Acres of the same Land; which is absurd, an infinity of unites being equal to an infinity of thousands.

Petty clearly recognizes that time preference, meaning our taste for impatience, explains productivity, or ratio of output to capital, rather than the other way around. This powerful and counterintuitive insight anticipates Böhm-Bawerk in 1889, whose achievement was to spell out the logic. The utility or *usus fructus* being a given, we bid less for the land or other capital producing it if we are less patient, and more if more. Bidding less for this denominator of rate of return bids that rate itself up if the numerator is a given, and conversely. That's why riskier assets offer higher return. Petty's *reductio ad absurdum* of a hypothesis of infinite patience is obvious in hindsight, but may not have been written down before. Petty continues:

Wherefore we must pitch upon some limited number, and that I apprehend to be the number of years, which I conceive one man of fifty years old, another of twenty eight, and another of seven years old, all being alive together may be thought to live; that is to say, of a Grandfather, Father and Childe; few men having reason to take care of more remote Posterity: for if a man be a great Grandfather, he himself is so much nearer his end, so as there are but three in a continual line of descent usually coexisting together; and as some are Grandfathers at forty years, yet as many are not till above sixty, and sic de etceteris.

20. Wherefore I pitch the number of years purchase, that any Land is naturally worth, to be the ordinary extent of three such person their lives. Now in England we esteem three lives equal to one and twenty years, and consequently the value of Land, to be about the same number of years purchase. Possibly if they thought themselves mistaken . . . .(as the observer on the Bills of Mortality thinks they are . . .)

21. . . . . But in other Countreys Lands are worth nearer thirty years purchase, by reason of the better titles, more people, and perhaps truer opinion of the value and duration of three lives.

23. One the other hand, Lands are worth fewer years purchase (as in Ireland) . . . by reason of the frequent rebellions . . ."

The "other Countreys" would include France and especially Holland, then models of prosperity. Petty had made his fortune in Irish mortgages, where conditions were opposite, and knew the years purchase there.

The argument is a puzzle. There is a focus on longevity and mortality, as if the generations are providing for old age. But Petty's overlapping generations model cannot be much like Paul Samuelson's of three centuries later, where a generation of productives leaves a nest egg for retirement. Samuelson's productives are replenished exogenously, with children left to the imagination. Why would Petty have mentioned their ages? And retirement at age 50, as a norm, would have made no sense to Petty or his readers. The grandfather will stay in harness.

The one and twenty years could mean remaining life expectancy at age 50. But Petty could easily have spelled that out, or the implied 71-year terminus. He does spell out the ages of the three generations. Their average difference in age rounds to 21 years.

Petty's readers, like Smith's and Ricardo's after, would have taken it for granted that each generation provides for the next. "Few men having reason to take care of more remote posterity" would have registered in the context of that provision. "Posterity" usually meant and means descendants.

His description, like mine, is incomplete. He may mean that life expectancy is also a factor in calculating the years purchase. If so, he apparently leaves that thought to be followed up later. There is also room to argue that the grandfather looks two generations ahead, so that the years purchase becomes 42 years. But that would give the *usus fructus* at 2.3%. All the rates Petty reports elsewhere in the tract are much higher. One generation length is what he seems to apply. My reading is that the grandfather provides for the grandson by passing all to the son.

Petty's overlapping generation insight has been one of his least noticed, just as with Mill's on output growth preceding and explaining capital growth. I first read of Petty's idea in a collection of Lionel Robbins' lectures at London School of Economics delivered in 1979–1980, but published in 2000. I learned from these lectures that Gustav Cassel had published the same idea in his *The Nature and Necessity of Interest* in 1903. I hunted that down. Robbins misremembered in telling his students that Cassel had arrived at the idea independently. In fact Cassel and Robbins both quote the same excerpts from *A Treatise of Taxes* that I just did. Cassel inferred that interest rates cannot stably be less than 2% per year.

I arrived at the same idea independently, anyhow, and published it in *Social Science Information* in 1989. To date it is my only publication in a refereed journal. Alan Rogers, a population geneticist teaching at the University of Utah, published almost the same idea in 1994[3] and 1997.[4] Neither of us knew of Petty or Cassel or each other. Both of Rogers' two papers are reproduced at my website (logicandeconomics.com). Alan is a much better economist than I am, although neither claims any credentials in the field, and I will let his papers speak for themselves. Petty's great idea has otherwise remained unnoticed as far as I know.

His idea in modern terms comes from the same ancient capitalization formula. Sumerian temples knew how to evaluate land, as well as mortgages and annuities, by discounting to present value. In the simplest case, where cash flow is

---

[3] *The Evolution of Time Preference.*
[4] *Evolution and Human Choice over Time.*

expected to hold constant forever, the logic begins with the definition of cash flow rate as cash flow divided by capital. Then capital, by implication, equals cash flow divided by cash flow rate. "Years purchase" meant the reciprocal of cash flow rate, if assumed to be steady, so that we could say that capital such as the cornfield was worth its predicted cash flow times so many years purchase.

Where capital is constant over time, cash flow and cash flow rate become identical to output (cash flow plus capital growth by the total return truism) and rate of return. Sumerians realized that return is the universal maximand, three millennia before Turgot wrote that down, and that competition tended to equalize it to a current market norm. In growthlessness, it would also equal the reciprocal of years purchase.

Petty was searching for the rationale of years purchase, and found it in the generation length. Petty's idea I think, and mine anyhow, could begin with a concept of capital as a means of accomplishing goals. His key assumption, accepted more or less throughout the classical school he founded, is that our overriding goal is lineage survival. My approach to this idea loosely equates the biological concept of fitness, or means of lineage survival, to the economic one of total capital as our means to carry out our purposes. They are the same insofar as lineage survival is our recognized or unrecognized guiding purpose.

Nature's way seems to be transmission of all fitness, meaning total capital for humans, to the next generation. Nature cares just as much for later generations, but trusts each generation of immediate descendants to know best what their own immediate descendants will need for that long-range goal. Each passes the baton and withdraws. We invest everything in the next generation precisely because we care about the ones after. Petty, if I understand him, follows that idea. I think he means that years purchase converges to the generation length. The reciprocal of 21 years, which he took as the generation length as I read him, comes to 4.8% per year (i.e., $\frac{1}{21} = .048$). Then the cash flow rate, which simplifies to the pure consumption rate at the collective scale, would come to 4.8% per year. This would tally well enough with rates of return and interest rates as Petty knew them.

I would adjust Petty's estimate of the generation length. Petty's primogeniture model may have been true to law and custom for land inheritance, but it is not true to biology. I prefer R. A. Fisher's[5] method equal-weighting all births from first to last, and equal-weighing ages of both parents at each birth. We have some evidence that the maternal generation length, by that method, has run near 26 years over recent decades. If fathers are five years older on average, Fisher's method would arrive at 28.5 years. Rogers found 28.9 years from other sources. The reciprocal of 28.5 years is 3.5% per year.

My 3.5% is a rough estimate. What counts is the generation length. The length was probably higher, and the rate lower, before medicine and sanitation lowered mortality

---

[5] *The Genetical Theory of Natural Selection* (1930).

rates, and let two or three births per couple meet the need for population replenishment.

The cash flow or pure consumption rate modeled at 3.5% might also vary for reasons other than changes in the generation length. My charts show the pure consumption ratio (pure consumption/total capital) in the middle part of the twentieth century at approximately double the long-term norm, as people drained capital reserves to keep up consumption in times of world depression and world war. This reflects what I call the Piketty U-curve dropping physical capital and profit compared to other variables in those hard times. My 3.5% is proposed as an elastic norm, not a rigid one, for the pure consumption ratio.

Rate of return, by the truism, is that plus growth rate. I model growth as free, trusting the free growth rule and the evidence supporting it in charts and tables.

FIRST INTERPRETATION

Next generation theory says in effect that R. A. Fisher's version of the generation length, not Petty's primogeniture version, gives the period of production of total capital. We would miss the point if we focused on the period of production of human capital separately. *Total* capital is our means of lineage survival. This reinforces my theme that human capital does not mean humans. It means skill sets priced at present value of foreseen cash flow to ourselves as the only possible owners. Skill sets are not enough for lineage survival. We also need things. We should not fall into the trap of surplus value theory, which had been taught by communists for decades before Marx joined their ranks, in supposing that skills make things. It is only half the truth. Skills plus things make skills plus things as the generations repeat.

Nor should we make the mistake of supposing that the generation length begins and ends uniquely from birth to birth, so that the remaining period of production grows shorter over adult life and the time discount rate steeper. The period of a cycle is the same at any point. Each generation as a whole produces the next as a whole. Each cohort (same-age set) completes its role with production of its counterpart in the next. The cohort of eight-year-olds, by investing directly in themselves, invest indirectly in the next generation of eight-year-olds. That's why Fisher's version of the generation length is better than those which consider only the male or female generation length, or consider firstborns only as in Petty's model. Fisher's version prioritizes each cohort and gender equally, without judgment as to which matter more. The period of production gives our patience horizon. The horizon and its reciprocal, the pure consumption ratio, both hold the same at any age.

DON'T GRANDPARENTS INVEST?

Next generation theory assumes that each generation invests all its capital of both factors in the next within the generation length. We expect it to do the same in turn. We care about grandchildren too, but serve them best by trusting and enabling their parents only.

A first reaction is that this denies the obvious. Humans today, in advanced countries, normally live to nearly three times the generation length. (3 x 28.5 = 85.5). And job number one for grandparents seems to be helping take care of grandchildren. Doesn't that falsify next generation theory?

Not quite. Retirement typically means dependence on savings or subsidy. The parental generation subsidizes both the young and the old. Retirees can be interpreted to some extent as hired though willing caregivers paid for by parents. Parents are the real investors, in this case, and grandparents the willing mediaries.

That explains part. The rest, I think, is best explained as replenishing a capital reserve. I mentioned that nature builds up reserves in good times and depletes them in bad times. A rise in longevity from what is normally needed for lineage survival is a rise in human capital reserves. Human capital is the most versatile kind. We geezers have lost a step. But we remember how it's done. We particularly remember how parenting and homemaking are done, since those change least with technology. Julius Caesar's nanny, with a few pointers and sign language, could probably fill in as a nanny today. If the parental generation were pulled away to fight a war, or rebuild after a catastrophe, we oldsters could keep up the home front.

CASH FLOW AND RISK

Next generation theory can now be tested against the data. But since the theory predicts total capital cash flow rate, while the data show physical capital cash flow rate only, we will need to know something about the difference.

Tradition recognizes that time preference and return vary with risk. Return is growth rate plus cash flow rate. Is the risk premium captured more in one of these two components than the other? We might intuit that riskier and higher-return assets grow faster on average, over enough time for the bumps of risk to even out. But if that tended to be true, the universe of assets would grow progressively riskier over the decades and centuries. That isn't what I see. Then the risk premium tends to be expressed in cash flow rate rather than growth rate.

For illustration, consider factor risk. I argued that human capital figures to be the riskier and higher-return factor because assets tend to reflect the risk appetites of their owners. The young are more risk-tolerant, and own human capital disproportionately. If this higher return were reflected in higher growth, rather than in higher cash flow, the ratio of human to physical capital would tend to rise steadily over the millennia. Most readings have tended to see it the other way around. I myself favor the neutral assumption that the factors keep pace. Then cash flow rate becomes higher for human than physical capital, with 3.5% the cap-weighted average.

The history of corporate leverage shows the same. Equities are riskier because bond interest is paid first. If equities grew faster, however, leverage would constantly decline. That too is not what we see.

This inferred concentration of risk premium in cash flow rate is convenient for testing. Growth and return are two of the most closely followed variables in economics. Cash flow is the difference. We have no direct measure of the pure consumption rate, or cash flow rate at the collective scale. Nor have we any direct measure of growth and return to total capital at any scale. But we have a good idea of *average* return and growth and cash flow to securities and business assets. Average rates give aggregate ones. And return to human capital, by the maximand rule, should tend to be the same as with physical capital but for differences in risk. I model human capital as somewhat riskier, from the owner rule, and human capital is the larger as well as the riskier and higher-return factor. Then if I am right in placing the risk premium within the cash flow component of return, and in estimating average-risk cash flow rate at 3.5%, cash flow rate to the business sector as a whole should be somewhat less.

TESTING NEXT GENERATION THEORY

The proxies for the pure consumption ratio in security markets would be dividend yield for equities, and interest for debt claims. Ibbotson Associates' SBII (2012), Chapter 4, shows average real interest on U.S. corporate bonds as

3.0% over the period 1926–2011. Real corporate dividend yield rate over the period can be estimated from the same source at about 2.9%. Jeremy Siegel's *Stocks for the Long Run* (2002), Table 1–2, reports data extending back to 1802. Real return over the period 1802–2001 is shown as averaging 3.5% for long-term governments, and 2.9% for short-term governments. Corporate bond returns would have run somewhat higher.

Global Financial Data shows stock market information for 95 countries. Data for U.K., U.S., Germany, Australia and France begin from 1701, 1801, 1870, 1883 and 1896 respectively. My website *logicandeconomics.com* shows this information along with evidence for free growth.

The eighteenth century is represented by U.K. alone. U.K. then showed real price return, dividend yield and total return at 21.4%, 7.9% and 29.3%. Volatility of dividend yield was exceptional. That dividend rate is more than double the 3.5% I model. But it would be more or less as expected if the eighteenth century is interpreted as something like the twentieth. Both were centuries of war and revolution. Piketty's data show that consumption/market-valued capital ratios rose to roughly double the norm in some countries in the twentieth century. The same might be true of the eighteenth.

From 1801 forward, U.K. averages for these flows were 2.2%, 4.2% and 6.4%. U.S. figures from 1801 forward were 2.9%, 5.3% and 8.3%. *Global Financial Data* also shows collective flows for Europe and the world since 1926. Here the figures were 3.3%, 3.9% and 7.3% for Europe, and 3.5%, 3.8% and 7.3% for the world.

Modeling of the pure consumption ratio before the emergence of stock markets could refer to the history of interest rates alone. Interest is rate of return to senior claims. Rate of return to any claim is realization by investors net of all expense. Investors in debt claims means lenders, not borrowers. Interest rates published historically are rates borrowers are contracted to pay. Interest rates realized by lenders are less for two reasons. There are friction costs of due diligence, contracting and collection. Default costs, slight when times are good, can be catastrophic when times are bad.

Sidney Homer and Richard Sylla describe normal contractual rates, not realized rates net of those costs, as 10%–40% in Sumer and Babylonia, 6%–18% in ancient Greece, 5%–24% in Egypt, and 4%–12+% in Rome and the Byzantine Empire.[6] After higher rates in the dark ages, European mortgages and commercial loans found the range 7%–25% in the thirteenth and fourteenth centuries.[7] The range settled down to 4%–14% in the sixteenth century,[8] and to 3%–10% by the seventeenth and eighteenth.[9] The authors comment:[10] "... interest rates declined during much of the later Middle Ages and Renaissance. The earliest short-term rates quoted were somewhat higher than the last

---

[6] *A History of Interest Rates*, Rutgers, 1996, Table 4.
[7] Ibid. Tables 6 and 7.
[8] Ibid. Table 9.
[9] Ibid. Tables 10 and 14.
[10] Ibid. Chapter 10.

and highest of the western Roman legal limits. They were not too different from early Greek rates and were within the range of Babylonian rates ... The later Renaissance rates were well within the range of modern rates and the lowest were far below modern rates in periods of credit stringency." Merchants of Venice in Shakespeare's time and long before borrowed from banks, not from Shylocks, and at rather lower cost than merchants of the twentieth century.

SUMMARY

Next generation theory trades my wannabe economist hat for my wannabe biologist one. The philosopher Herbert Spencer, in Darwin's time, called those fields the same at bottom. I never read Spencer, and know him mostly from Bertrand Russell's books on the history of philosophy. Spencer rates a subchapter there. Yet he was an autodidact with less training in either field than mine. He even had less training in philosophy than mine. He was a philosopher all the same, by Russell's tough standards, and knew that logic comes first. Data eventually prove their worth when it's time to test. The data I've found fits next generation theory more or less. What I really have on, all the while, is my wannabe philosopher hat.

Next generation theory is a blockbuster. Wars have been fought as to whether interest and return can be justified at all. Even today, many agree with Schumpeter that return naturally converges to zero in the stationary state (growthlessness), and generally to the growth rate. Next generation theory and the data say that it varies around a norm of about 3.5% per year plus whatever the total capital growth rate proves to be.

6

MACRO

I said that macro as taught today has meant strategies to reconcile price stability with full employment of plant and labor at the national scale. A Keynesian approach emphasizes government intervention through fiscal and monetary policy as described in Chapter 1. An anti-Keynesian one mistrusts intervention as doing more harm than good. Both schools, even so, are founded on Keynesian concepts of what basic terms mean. One of the aims of this book has been to disprove the Y or $Y = I + C$ doctrine that both accept as an article of faith. This chapter is about that and other ways for logic to reshape assumptions in macro.

CROWDING IN AND OUT

Everything in Keynesian analysis, and so in macro today, misses the elephant in the room. The elephant is productivity, or equivalently rate of return on capital of both factors. Return, I claim, is what the interventionists and anti-interventionists are really arguing about. The proper focus is "social" return to the electorate, including indirect return when a policy stimulates private investment. That stimulation is called "crowding in." Crowding in will happen whenever investors foresee value added.

Monetary policy has provided weak medicine for hard times because interest rate cuts add too little to investment attractiveness. Fiscal policy to improve infrastructure (say roads and bridges) is a much more promising approach if made to act fast enough. There is little crowding out, meaning lowering prospective return to private investment, because private investors do not normally own roads and bridges so as to have invested in them instead. There is crowding in because better infrastructure means faster and cheaper results, translating to higher returns, at every stage in production and marketing.

One popular anti-Keynesian (anti-interventionist) doctrine is Nobelist Robert Lucas's "rational expectations": tax cuts will stay unspent because taxpayers will maintain liquidity to meet foreseen restoration of the taxes later. This analysis is not wrong, but again misses the key variable of return. Investment in a slump risks negative return. Money in vaults, returning the comfort of liquidity if nothing else, is the easy choice. There are often circumstances where keeping money unspent gives the best return available. The maximand rule affirms that most will choose it. A few including my father have seen opportunity worth the risk, in the world depression for instance, and have brought what others sell at distress prices. Most preferred the sidelines. Recessions and depressions are cured not with tax cuts and cheap money, but with better investment prospects. When rational expectations are of high return, investment crowds in.

MACRO TODAY AND TOMORROW

Macro, or the art of managing national economies, is as old as government. Its history is a history of crisis management. Navigation between inflation and recession has proved tricky because avoiding one has seemed to risk the other. Monetary policy, which controls interest rates and the money supply, invites government to name its poison. I said that I see neither logic nor evidence that it cures unemployment, and that the same goes for tax cuts. Money stays in pockets, and prefers zero return over negative return, until better prospects crowd investment in.

Chapter 1 presented my idea of what macro might mean tomorrow. Let's go through it again. Over the next few decades, commercial banks should devolve into deposit banks investing in ETFs and mutual funds on the one side, and lending banks raising funds from shareholders or term lenders on the other. Government should do nothing to prevent this devolution. It will end the 10:1 leverage (deposit/equity) which has brought down the banking system about once per generation, by my assessment, for the past eight centuries. Transaction money will remain currency and bank deposits, but those deposits will now earn full market return as inducement for account owners to remain invested rather than spend. This idea is what I called market money. The tightrope walk between too much and too little in circulation goes away when market money becomes the norm. It burns no holes in pockets if it yields market return as long as we hold it.

It seems to me that bank devolution should bring higher interest rates as investors demand return, and that market efficiency should respond with a shift from debt to equity financing. Firms can sell new stock issues to retire structural debt, and newlyweds can rent, rather than borrow to buy, as I said in Chapter 1, until incomes double by their mid-thirties or so.

Fiscal policy works when government invests to maximize social return, including effects of crowding in, just as corporate investment aims to maximize return to shareholders. Roads and bridges should go not where the jobs are needed, and not where the votes are needed, but where the roads and bridges are needed. It should not wait for slumps to cure, but should rather help prevent them by timely investment in infrastructure or other needs which the free market lacks means or motive to fill.

Bank devolution and market money should tend to dissociate and alleviate the challenges of underemployment/ overemployment and money value instability, although some of both will be with us forever. That does not mean that macro will have worked its way out of a job. The future of macro, in my guess, lies mostly in expanding, refocusing and interpreting national accounts to gain a clearer picture of national wealth, national output and factor incomes. I'll get to those soon.

MARKET MONEY

What I called market money in Chapter 1 is not particularly my idea unless in details. The old problem it addresses is how to reconcile all the qualities wanted in money while containing the risk of inflation traditionally associated with oversupply. Market money finds the solution: there can be no oversupply of investment opportunities offering competitive risk-adjusted return. ETFs meet that test while offering the instant liquidity that is the essence of money. They trade in seconds, during market hours, at current quotes for the underlying securities. This valuation method gives "net asset value" or NAV. Mutual funds, tradable ("redeemable") in a day or so at NAV, can also serve. Either option offers risk/ return to taste. Dollars remain the measure of value and medium of exchange. ETFs are the repositories or stores of wealth convertible into dollars at a moment's notice. As such they compete with banks, until banks also invest in ETFs rather than in term loans as now.

The chief advantage of market money is to free the money supply to increase without risk of overspending and inflation. Money today burns holes in pockets because it earns nothing but the comfort of liquidity until spent. Market money earns that comfort too, and competitive return for every risk appetite as well.

Say that a bank devolves, as I expect all will, into deposit banks and lending banks with different shareholders and essentially no interaction. Deposit banks might invest each account into treasury or SPDR ETFs, or any mix, as directed by the depositor to suit her risk tolerance. These two popular options might be enough. Depositors are typically not sophisticated investors seeking the added benefits and added costs of managed portfolios, and anyhow most studies show that benefits of professional portfolio management do not outweigh those costs. Since prices of these ETFs and others are published continually online, the deposit bank knows the value of each account in real time. This means that electronic payments from any accounts can be limited to that value, so that merchants accepting those payments can be assured of full and instantaneous coverage. That is not the general rule in bank payments today.

This gives an idea of why I think deposit-and-lend banks cannot survive. Their deposit function has no chance against market money. Even their lending function is losing ground to crowdsourcing alternatives. The world can do without their 10:1 leverage and the eight centuries of crisis it has cost. Now let's go over some of the features of market money in detail.

PAYMENT MEDIATION

Banks effect payments from depositors' accounts. ETF accounts can do the same. All these payments can be electronic. A payer, typically a customer, might swipe a card or click a screen. A payee, typically a vendor, typically must verify first that the account is authentic and covers the payment offered. An ETF fund could be well-suited to give this quick transparency.

First, it can be essentially an index fund. It can be composed of a published ratio of index ETFs and index mutual funds, say of SPDRs and Treasuries. The fund can track all these indexes online, and knows from tick to tick what each account is worth. So long as management effects all payments in and out, and constructs each account of index exposures itself, and tracks those exposures and payments in real time, it knows account values exactly.

Risk-tolerant clients who choose investment in SPDRs will expect daily ups and downs in account size. That means that they will have to carry larger accounts in order to be sure of covering payments in the downswings. They can afford to do so with no sacrifice of return because market money effectively keeps them invested.

WHY INVEST IN INDEXES?

On sound microeconomic principle, professional asset management will add value over index results before deduction of fees. Otherwise they couldn't stay in business. The same principle says that the fees will converge to that pre-fee value added. Price converges to marginal utility (value). In less technical language, services including money management tend to be worth neither more nor less than what they cost. Investors bid fees up when fees are less, and down when they are more. As a rule of thumb, investors should expect to do equally well in managed or index accounts when fee costs are considered as well.

The market forces that make this so are worth a look. Managed and index funds compete in a kind of density-dependent flux like hawks and doves in game theory. It pays to be a hawk when the hawk/dove ratio is too low, and a dove when too high. When hawks have only hawks to fight, they will win only half the time. Fighting becomes a losing strategy when it risks more than winning stands to gain. More doves will mean easier contests.

So it is with asset managers: Index funds (doves) avoid commitment (fights) as to which firms and sectors will outperform. This neutrality saves the costs of research needed for commitment. Asset managers (hawks) pay those costs and recover them when outperformance results. That means outperforming the index. But if asset managers collectively managed the whole market, they would become the index. Some would outperform others, but the whole group cannot outperform itself. Then it could not recover its research costs. Many would have to close their doors, leaving the field to index funds which don't pay those costs, until market equilibrium was restored.

Then what determines equilibrium? Is the critical variable percent of trades by managed funds? I thought so for a while. Now I think it's percent of AUM (market value of assets under management). My reasoning now is that holds by portfolio managers reveal informed opinion on security values as clearly as trades do. Research cost is the same for both. If a manager neither buys nor sells, she tells us that she thinks the price is right. The critical variable is not trade volume, but percent of aggregate market cap of the whole economy controlled by asset managers collectively. When professionals manage more than some critical percent of the whole economy, yet to be determined, it is time to switch from managed to index funds.

The number of asset managers is much less critical. There must be enough of them for competition within each specialty or sector of investment. Too many is not a concern. Abler ones, on microeconomic principle, will displace the less able. That's why Spencer taught that natural selection works the same in economics as in biology.

Market money is for everyone as an investor as well as a payer. Very few people have the time or training to play hawk and try to beat the market. I myself have neither. What we have is a sense of our degree of risk-aversion. An ETF fund gives the broadest and most flexible coverage of risk appetites. It can poll and advise clients on risk preferences, and invest in Treasuries or SPDRs to suit.

HOW MARKET MONEY MIGHT EVOLVE

Market money exists today in the form of ETF and mutual fund[1] accounts. If I were a few decades younger, I might push the idea by joining in. I would probably start with ETFs

---

[1]   These include "money market" funds investing in short debt instruments. Market money includes these along with the rest of the ETF and mutual fund universe.

155

alone, for instant liquidity at current prices visible online, and specifically SPDR and Treasury ETFs for lowest trading costs. The focus would be on providing bank-like payment services, and on bettering the banks in them from the start. The target clientele would be the world of depositors rather than sophisticated investors.

It seems to me that banks as we know them today could not offer much competition. Demand deposits typically pay no interest, and would process payments no better. Market money offers a continuous range of returns according to client tolerance for risk.

Banks offer the advantage of federal deposit insurance (FDIC). It will not be enough. The market money fund carries no debt in itself, and needs no insurance. As it grows, banks will take notice. They can keep up the uneven fight, or they can join the parade. My working assumption is that many will prefer the latter. Banks are well-positioned to make the most of the idea. They have the needed expertise and systems and clientele in place. They can spin off their lending from their deposit operations as separate ventures to find lending capital from investors rather than depositors.

If there were no FDIC, there would be no deposits and no commercial banks. People can read the newspapers. Anyone old enough has lived through periodic bailouts. I'm a free-market fan who dislikes FDIC. But we would be rash to yank the rug from under banks by repealing it. We shouldn't even hint that we might. The world we know is built around banks, and banks are built on FDIC. Let it stand. How can anyone know for sure that money market and independent lending banks will do better? I think they will despite that advantage for banks.

A New Approach to Monetary Policy

Market money alone does not guarantee price stability. Commodity prices might still vary for whatever reason. Market money remains dollar-denominated, and dollars in themselves might still inflate or deflate. Then how can prices be kept steady if and when market money becomes the norm? That's where my real dollars idea fits in. Let's give it a closer look.

TIPS, in investment lingo, means Treasury Inflation-Protected Securities. If their coupon rate is 2%, and inflation turns out to be 1%, you get the sum or 3% in current dollars. My monetary policy idea might be called dollars inflation-protected or DIPS.

Let's imagine the mechanics. Government assumes a DIPS policy effective from 1/1/2020. Real dollars start as equal to nominal dollars at that moment. Suppose that inflation proves a steady 1%. For example, I buy dinner on 1/1/2021. The tab shows $100. I pay in greenbacks just as today. But I pay $101 in these nominal dollars to keep up with inflation. If there were 1% deflation instead, I would pay $99. (The algebra is actually a little different to reflect compounding.)

The default assumption here is that prices are posted in real dollars. This saves vendors such as the restaurant the risks and headaches of re-pricing, called "menu change costs," when inflation or deflation would otherwise have forced them. Since DIPS are legal tender from 1/1/2020 on, the vendor must accept them when prices are posted in dollars. That's what legal tender means. But he is free to post them in nominal dollars or zlotys or what he likes. Suppose the symbol $N is agreed to mean nominal dollars. If the posted price is $N100 at the restaurant, I pay $100 in greenbacks.

The same rules apply in card or electronic payments. If the credit card company shows that I owe them $100, that means 101 nominal dollars in the 1% inflation case. If I pay by smart card and still show a credit balance of $N500 because that's what the smart card company prefers, then my credit is 500 nominal dollars or greenbacks.

This gives the main idea. Inflation or deflation continues as it will, in the sense that nominal dollars might hold any proportion to real dollars as the future rolls on. DIPS insulate and immunize the economy from most practical effects. Apps in our cell phones keep up with the conversion rate and do the math.

Does that mean that DIPS do no more than sweep inflation under the rug? Yes. Let it pile to the moon if that's what happens. The economy works on top of the rug. It shrugs off inflation and deflation as it buys and sells in DIPS. Nor need piling to the moon be expected. I personally sense a momentum toward bank devolution, world de-leveraging and market money. I have trouble visualizing what could drive sustained inflation or deflation when money burns no holes in pockets and business cycles are not amplified by debt. My hunch, at that point, lies more toward a random drift in nominal dollar value up or down. I would expect inflation to pile under the rug until then.

This analysis shows that market money and DIPS are independent ideas. Neither implies the other. Market money cannot well become the norm before bank devolution. DIPS can happen now. I see no reason why they shouldn't.

THE POTENTIAL OF NATIONAL ACCOUNTS

National accounts are doing almost nothing wrong. They must re-think the Capital Consumption Adjustment (CCAdj) which models depreciation as decreasing rather than rising exponentially. That aside, my critique found only opportunities missed.

It is time for an expansion of their purview and a reconsideration of their focus. As to focus, accountancy is best at reporting cash flow. Depreciation accounting, even in its most sophisticated form used in national accounts, is a sorry substitute for mark-to-market measures when available. That is the plight and opportunity of macro. It sees through a glass darkly now because it sees outdated information on capital and capital growth (net investment). Balance sheets get the news of outside reality piecemeal as new materials are bought and products sold. That can stop now. National accounts can report market-valued capital growth side by side with book net investment, and let the world choose.

What I would choose, hands down, is market measures. Consumption plus market-valued capital growth, not plus book net investment, is what I track as $Y = I + C$ in the charts and tables. But that still tells us only about output before applying the asterisks, and I have found no way to apply them better than a crude estimate in the three-fourths rule. That's why I suggest a shift in focus for national accounts.

The focus now is gross product, domestic or national. (Domestic means made in the nation, whether by nationals or not, while national means made anywhere by nationals.) It can be proved from definitions that gross product equals "expenditure," or gross realized output of both factors plus proprietary profit. Expenditure is well worth tracking. But it seems to me that *net* product, domestic or national, reveals little of interest. Its consumption and investment components are interesting separately, if investment is measured as growth in market-valued capital, but their sum even then is a poor measure of output. I would continue to report it for tradition's sake, while shifting focus to pay, consumption and market-valued capital as more directly measurable and of more heuristic use.

National accounts should risk more imputation and interpretation. This is the expansion of purview I'd like to see. The purview now is pretty much pure accountancy. We need that, but we need more too. I will argue, for example, that we could benefit from a fuller picture of consumption and pay than pure accountancy is likely to provide. I think economists and accountants together could provide enough through imputation.

The aim would be to stimulate debate, not to foreclose it. What imputations and interpretations make the most sense?

What share of proprietorship and partnership revenue should be interpreted as pay? How much should be imputed to the self-employed at home? How much consumption is Schultz's pure kind, and how much his invested kind? Let everyone weigh in. Of course there are different understandings of economics, and even of accounting. And my suggestions for change in focus are not the only defensible ones. I will first try to show how more fullness and detail in reporting consumption could be helpful.

NATIONAL WEALTH INCLUDING HUMAN CAPITAL

By definition, pure consumption ratio is pure consumption divided by total capital. This can be arranged as what I call the total capital truism: total capital equals pure consumption divided by the pure consumption ratio. Next generation theory argues from the biological imperative that the pure consumption ratio tends toward 3.5% per year for humans at the collective scale. Historical data given in the last chapter showed dividend and interest rates as more or less in this region since Sumerian times, with the qualifier that interest can rise substantially in sustained hard times and return to the norm in recoveries.

The three-fourths rule models pure consumption as about three-fourths of all consumption. Consumption, in national accounts, shows as personal consumption expenditure (PCE) plus government consumption expenditure (GCE). GCE includes government outlays, at all levels of government, on education and welfare. These are easily recognized as consumption. It also includes costs of law enforcement, national defense, fire control, and maintenance of infrastructure such as highways and water systems and government buildings. These too count as consumption, even if we mightn't have thought so. They are part of the cost of our survival. That's why I agree with Kuznets and tradition, although I didn't always, that consumption includes all of GCE as well as PCE.

PCE in the United States in 2015 shows as $12.429 trillion. GCE is reported at $2.5855 trillion. Both are in 2015 dollars. Their sum is $15.0145 trillion. Three-fourths of that is $11.2609 trillion. Then the truism, trusting national accounts and the three-fourths rule, would divide $11.2609 trillion by 3.5% to get $321.74 trillion for total capital of the U.S. in 2015 in dollars of that year.

This estimate is rough because of uncertainties in both numerator and denominator. We don't really know the size of pure consumption, and we deduce the pure consumption ratio only as an elastic norm which might double in sustained hard times. With those caveats, it can be borne in mind when we evaluate the tax base and the risk of national debt. National accounts (flow of funds reports) show the sum of private and public debt as $45,157.5 trillion in 2015. I add bank deposits of $14.6846 trillion to find U.S. total debt at $59.8421 trillion, or some 18.6% of total capital. My impression is that this exposure is not yet dangerous. But it needs watching.

NATIONAL OUTPUT

Collective output, by the total return truism, adds change in total capital to pure consumption. We might find this by estimating national total capital as above from year to year, and adding the yearly change to our best measure of pure consumption.

NATIONAL PROFIT

The physical cash flow rule can make national profit particularly accessible in national accounts insofar as we can improve descriptions there of pay as well as consumption. The rule says that collective physical cash flow equals the second less the first. The total return truism shows that collective profit, as the output of physical capital, equals that difference plus change in market-valued capital. This means that we need only improve our measurements and imputations of pay, consumption and market-valued capital to calculate collective profit.

There is no need here to distinguish pure from invested consumption, as only their sum is needed. But we must push past the comfort zone of pure accounting to disentangle the components of pay and profit in proprietorships and partnerships, and to impute pay and consumption in voluntary household services.

SUMMARY AND DISCUSSION

The future of macro includes bank devolution. Deposit-and-land banks need deposit/equity leverage of at least 10:1. They must fail in high winds. Market forces should lead them to devolve into unaffiliated deposit and lending banks. Deposits would be invested in ETFs and mutual funds to combine market return with quick liquidity. Lending banks would lend money they own or borrow long-term.

Interest rates would figure to rise as lenders seeking competitive return replace depositors expecting none. As they rise, traditional borrowers will look more to equity financing. Newlyweds will rent rather than buy. Firms will raise new stock issues to replace structural debt.

Macro, or the art of reconciling full employment with dollar stability, will find its task easier. Medicine for one, in the world we know, can undercut the other. Bank devolution should help make those goals more separable and more tractable. Market money, meaning spendable liquidity with full market return tailored to risk appetite, can reach any supply without inflation risk. Deleveraging, meanwhile, should tend to moderate the business cycle.

Not all reforms in macro need await bank devolution. I concede that I am a certifiable "DIPSomaniac" who has no objection to sweeping inflation under the rug until bank devolution and market money ease inflationary and deflationary pressures. The real dollar could become legal tender right now, with no more inconvenience than in paying Euros rather than pounds. Apps in cell phones would keep abreast of conversion rates and do the math.

Now is also the time to reconsider the methods and objectives of national accounts. Market-valued capital deserves a larger role. Net investment I can show alternatively as change in market-valued capital, and net product Y as that plus consumption. Let each economist choose. Net and gross product, however, need not remain the focus. True output in the sense of the Y rule is impractical to measure. There is more promise in equations whose variables are consumption, market-valued capital and pay. These are things we can actually measure. Economists could reveal more about consumption and pay by sophisticated interpretation of the raw numbers. We might gain a better idea of imputed pay in households, and of the shares of pay and profit in proprietorship income. We might also find ways to tease apart the pure and invested components of consumption, and to evaluate consumer durables in nations that don't report them now.

Accountancy measures. Economics interprets. Pure accounting, a beautiful thing in itself, is seldom meant as sufficient. National accounts have reflected some economic interpretation from the start. The future is in more, and in refocus to build on natural strengths.

NOTATION

THE TOTAL CAPITAL TRUISM

By definition, the pure consumption rate c_p is

$$c_p = \frac{C_p}{K_T},$$

where C_p is pure consumption and K_T (or V) is total capital H + K. Arrangement as

$$K_T = \frac{C_p}{c_p}$$

gives the total capital truism (true by definition). Next generation theory proposes $c_p \to 3.5\%$ / year as an elastic norm at the collective or universal scale. The three-fourths rule meanwhile estimates pure consumption as three-fourths of all consumption $C = C_p + C_s$. By those assumptions,

$$K_T \to \frac{.75C}{.0035/yr}.$$

National accounts gave C= PCE + GCE as $11.2609 trillion in 2015. That would put K_T at $321.74 trillion.

7

ADDENDA

This book was once to have been titled "Free Growth and Other Surprises." Just that. Feedback confirmed my worry that I hadn't shown a unifying theme. It began percolating through that the unifying theme is logic. I erase the blackboard, picking axioms and inferring consequences as if no one had tried that before. I worry about evidence at the end.

How dare I say that economics needed this rethinking from scratch? Math is the purest form of logic, and economics is the most math-intensive of the social studies. But math expressing careless doctrines only specifies the carelessness. Garbage in, garbage out. The Y doctrine, and the concomitant W one holding that pay measures work, are classic examples. The deadweight loss rule and maximand rule are certain. Both confirm the recovery rule. That dynamites the Y and W doctrines. Age-wage profiles add illustration, not proof, as no empirical proof is needed. The maintenance exhaust principle contradicting Quesnay, which completes the pay rule, is not certainty because it invokes the biological imperative. We may doubt that if we like.

Not that all economics needs rebuilding. I find little wrong with micro. I concede a few wrong interpretations of micro, such as the greed-is-good *homo economicus* one which loosely parallels selfish-gene models in biology. Genes are selfish in that the ones that best code traits for lineage survival are likeliest to survive. But it doesn't follow that selfishness is one of those traits. I'll go into that next in appraising Hamilton's rule.

God bless economics! I argue that growth theory and other things in macro need better foundations. So did the Tower of Pisa. The Tower of Pisa, to those who don't live in its shadow, is an artwork of immortal beauty. Nor should we grouse that it lacks modern amenities. Many share my diagnosis of macro as scarcely better than the lore of the priests in Karnak, who predicted how much and when to plant from the date and height of the spring flood on the Nile. Our leading indicators, like that one, are better than nothing. Erasing the blackboard is a step backward, not forward, unless we write something new.

BIOECONOMICS

PROBLEMS IN HAMILTON'S RULE

I discuss Hamilton's rule, in Chapter 1 and again here, because it is the elephant in the room of bioeconomics. Next generation theory barges into that room, if the maintenance exhaust principle hadn't already, and must critique that rule or leave the elephant out of the account. I critique it, as with the Y doctrine, out of respect for its adherents. Both are worth criticism precisely because wiser heads than mine accept them.

I'll boil my critique down to essentials. Chapter 1 showed the rule and a problem with the math. A hurdle rate of rB − C, where benefit B and cost C are fitness gained by the donee and fitness surrendered by the donor while r is relatedness between, implies a net gain in the transfer if relatedness is less than unity. The highest possible value of r without inbreeding in diploids such as us, where two parents contribute equal numbers of genes, is $\frac{1}{2}$. Then aggregate fitness of donor and donee together would have to grow by at least the amount of fitness the donor gave up: donee gained it at least twice while donor lost it once. The problem is that fitness means potential offspring, of ourselves or of our close kin, and more potential would tend to be expressed in more offspring. But populations aside from humans tend to fluctuate in size around zero over the millennia. So then must aggregate fitness.

Even so, Hamilton's rule gets some things right. Humans and other creatures *do* invest preferentially in close kin. We can see why to a point. Genes encode traits to replicate themselves because any that didn't weren't replicated. Hamilton's rule maximizes gene frequency, meaning percentage of the population showing that gene compared to its rivals at the same gene site, and so maximizes gene survival chances if frequency does. But Hamilton himself, ironically, would show how certain genes last longer by strategic withdrawal to *lower* frequencies at times when others can fill in for them to mutual advantage. It's like the quarterback trotting to the bench on fourth down because the time has come for other specialties on the field. We'll come back to that.

MATCHING

Recently (May 2017) I thought of something else. Two parents investing in two offspring that will survive to replace them would mean fitness transfer with neither gain nor loss. Dad and mom would each pass half their genes to two genic successors thanks to parallel motives and means of the two donors. This matching concept could fix the math in Hamilton's rule, while some other adjustment might allow the strategic withdrawal in frequency that Hamilton himself described later.

Matching need not be strictly in kind. Males in many species compete with other males in usually non-lethal tournaments or in displays. Females judge the winners, and mate preferentially with them. Sperm is cheap, since it contains none of the nutrients supplied in a female's eggs along with the same amount of genetic information, so that a few males can carry enough sperm to meet all female demand. That lets the few victorious fathers pair with the many mothers to start the next generation. The price of this gene shopping is that mothers are left pretty much alone to provide postnatal care. Losing males lack the genic motive, as they are unrelated, and winners are too few to provide much help. When fathers offer screened genes alone, as proved in the tournaments or displays, 1:1 matching in B/C can work only if gene screening provides as much fitness as care does. Suppose for the moment that it does.

Now the fun begins. Where at least three generations overlap, the simple case of two surviving offspring per breeding pair shows four grandparents equally motivated to invest in four grand-offspring, eight great-grandparents for eight grand-offspring, and so on indefinitely. Given any number of generations, we diploids (remember, that means two parents with two sets of chromosomes each) will tend to count as many ancestors going back that number as descendants going forward. That makes as many matchers, at any generational distance, as direct genetic heirs to receive. Relatedness halves with every step, but investment efficiency doubles as twice as many identically related matchers join in. A dollar's worth of grandma's genes now are traded for a dollar's worth of the very same genes two generations on, albeit dispersed among four donees. A dollar's worth of great-grandma's buys a dollar's worth dispersed over eight. Grandpa and great-grandpa get the same bargain. Given equally motivated matchers, as normally expected, we are motivated to invest at a B/C prospect of 1:1 in direct linear descendants at whatever generational remove.

At first glance, I have just blown up my own or Petty's next generation theory. The idea there is that we invest all resources in the first generation alone. But there is no contradiction. Matchers are equal in genic *motive,* but not in remaining fitness *means.* We invest in direct offspring first because no one is motivated to match us 1:1 except our mates and our living direct forbears. Forbears are a generation older at a minimum, and the fitness of each has been spent on the line leading to us. That leaves us and mate pretty much alone. Others will have motive and means only on exceptional occasions. Nor will we have grand-offspring unless offspring come first.

The truth needn't always be that simple. Populations could also survive in principle if each generation invested exclusively in the grand offspring one, say, once such a system got started. Next generation theory says that isn't how it works.

Nor are all creature diploids. Some social insects show one mother or queen lasting over many generations, plus a few drone fathers each contributing only half as many genes as she does, while generations of daughters (workers) invest in their progressively younger sisters as well as the new drones. Hamilton's rule predicted for them as well, and so must my variant when I come to it.

Investment in that case is between siblings (sibs), where relatedness is complicated by the fact that the queen contributes two thirds of the genes. For diploids such as us, again, relatedness between sibs without inbreeding is $\frac{1}{2}$. My simple model of two offspring per two parents gives no third sib to match the first, so that any investment from sib to sib must meet the 2:1 B/C standard expected by Hamilton. But investment in sib's offspring (relatedness=

$\frac{1}{4}$) finds an identically motivated matcher in sib's mate's sib. (Okay to take a few seconds on that one.) That means that each avuncle (uncle or aunt) is motivated to invest in each nepote (nephew or niece) at a B/C standard of 2:1, not 4:1 as per Hamilton's rule, because there is another avuncle of the same two nepotes to match. So it continues down the generations. Given that each individual has two avuncles in dad's one sib and mom's one sib, in my simple two-on-two model, each avuncle finds another to match. The same B/C standard of 2:1 that suffices for investment in sib suffices for nepotes or grand-nepotes or any of sib's descendants forever.

Next come first cousins. Relatedness here is $\frac{1}{8}$; $\frac{1}{2}$ to parent times $\frac{1}{2}$ to parent's sib times $\frac{1}{2}$ to either of parent's sib's two offspring. Each individual in the simple case has four first cousins in mom's sib's two offspring plus dad's sib's two. The one sib of each first cousin is an equally motivated matcher in investment in any of the four. That matching makes the B/C standard 4:1, rather than Hamilton's 8:1, for investment in first cousins. Again the same 4:1 standard, once determined, holds down the generations. Given two offspring per breeding pair, the number of potential donors holds proportion to the number of donees identically related to them.

In all these cases I find matchers only among donors related *identically* to donees. We are related *equally* to our sibs and parents by $\frac{1}{2}$. But I don't count sib's parents as matchers of investments by the other sib because that would count parental investment twice. We count everything once, and once only, when we limit matchers to individuals identical in *relationship* to donees, and not only in relatedness.

All this suggests that we could fix the math problem in Hamilton's rule if we account for matching. His revised criterion might show as rmB>C, where m is number of potential matchers showing identical relationship to donees. But that alone wouldn't fix all the math problem. Investment in collaterals such as nepotes would still call for a B/C standard greater than the 1:1 average implicit in stable populations. rmB exceeding C must be understood as a target, not a minimum hurdle condition.

A point to remember here is that adult fitness seeps away as we age.[1] Each day offers a day's worth of potential investment. Cost C is the day's worth of fitness steadily lapsing whether we invest it or not. We invest it in the best rmB prospects we can find within that time limit. rmB exceeds C on good days, and falls short on bad ones. That enables investment in collaterals within a framework of population stability (B/C $\Rightarrow$ 1).

But a further adjustment is called for. Bob Trivers's "reciprocal altruism"[2] lending fitness to non-kin, as extended by Richard Alexander and others to allow repayment by descendants to descendants, is a way of banking fitness.

---

[1]   R.A. Fisher's *The Genetical Theory of National Selection* (1930) models this steady loss of fitness with age in his "reproductive value" V(x). Although V(x) is described as remaining potential offspring at age x, it can be interpreted to include investment of care in offspring already produced.

[2]   *The Evolution of Reciprocal Altruism (1971).*

Humans also store their means in property investments, and so perhaps do other species such as birds or beavers or social insects that build habitations and infrastructures. We could let the symbol A mean net banking in the sense of fitness entrusted out, plus fitness repaid out, less fitness received in trust or repaid in. Then Hamilton's rule could be further adjusted to show as $rmB + A - C$. As each day's worth of fitness ticks away, banking gives another alternative to beat the clock.

The banking term A also allows the strategic withdrawal in frequency that I mentioned. The idea comes from Hamilton's parasite theory with Marlene Zuk[3] in 1982. "Histocompatibility" genes for response to pathogens and parasites, they argued, vary in frequency over time to meet varying strains of those invaders. Each side chases a moving target. Neither the strains nor the genes to meet them, as a rule, are driven to extinction. They linger indefinitely at low frequency until called forth again. The quarterback trots to the bench because he and the coach both know that substitution of special teams and then the defense will put him in the best position later.

My spin on the parasite theory, which I take as Hamilton's masterpiece, sees our histocompatibility genes as having figured that out. The rivals they displace will prove their saviors if preserved at low frequencies until their specialties are needed again. Agonistic competition, not lethal, tests which gene best meets the crisis now and which will be

---

[3] *Heritable True Fitness and Bright Birds: A Role for Parasites.*

saved for later. Group selection, in preserving defeated rivals for later, is enlightened gene selfishness or kin selection.

Meanwhile my proposed rmB>C criterion, putting A aside, makes different predictions from Hamilton's. Testing between them might be possible. I differ from Hamilton in proposing for example that we invest in ourselves, in our offspring and our grand-offspring at the same 1:1 B/C criterion where means allow. I agree that a 2:1 ratio applies to investment in sibs, but I expect the same 2:1 standard for investment in sib's children and grandchildren. I expect a 4:1 standard for first cousins, not 8:1, and then the same 4:1 for investment is a first-cousin's direct descendants forever.

I have said nothing about monitoring and cheating in the matching strategy because little remains to be said. Reciprocal altruism plays by the same rules. Many have noted that much reciprocal altruism is among close kin. That happens, for example, when we invest in sib or nepotes at a B/C prospect less than 2:1, or in first cousins or their descendants at a prospect less than 4:1. The advance here amounts to a partly collateralized loan. If the borrower defaults, the lender still has something.

Clearly I am not the first to take account of matching in investment strategies. Biologists are not blind. I may be the first to force the question of the math, and to show how matching makes different predictions from Hamilton's.

I hadn't thought this all the way through when I met Hamilton, through Bob Trivers, at a conference in Squaw Valley about 20 years ago. He was the absent-minded professor to perfection. Moody, distracted, profound. I told him that I thought his 1982 paper "complemented and qualified" his 1964 one. I half-expected him to take offence at the word "qualified." Not at all. He smiled, a rare thing for him, and said, "It's been a long search."

The parasites got the last laugh on him in Africa in 2002. He made it back from his research area to London, and died in hospital there. Bob Trivers called him the deepest thinker in the world. That couldn't be wrong by much.

The irony is that his most famous idea is the one that most needs fixing. My substitution of rm for r fixes the math problem and incorporates the role of matching, but what remains is still a strategy for maximizing gene frequency in generation after generation, come what may, unless something like my A term is included too. Maximizing frequencies might or might not maximize survival chances. It doesn't for the quarterback on fourth down, whose alternative to the bench is lopsided loss and the intensive care ward. This is not a wise career move.

There is enough kin selection, wherever we look, to confirm that as a good rule of thumb. No parent will doubt its predictive power. No one who owns a dog will swallow it whole. I fit both categories. That's why I chose the term "lineage survival" to accommodate whatever the rules of kin and group selection might prove to be.

WHY BIOLOGY AND ECONOMICS ARE PHILOSOPHY

Economics and evolutionary biology are much the same. Helen Keller, born blind and deaf, might still have reasoned her way through much of both. Hamlet would have loved them. I love them most when they test the limits of logic, and consult the data only at the end. The theme from which both reason, as Spencer[4] taught in the nineteenth century, is what he called "survival of the fittest." Karl Popper, a century later, disapproved of truism and found some here: we define fitness as potential survival, and then measure it as survival. Truism or tautology is in fact the ideal form of logic. Spencer's idea would be so much the more convincing if revealed as such. But it happens not to be. Measurement implies an "empirical" world of data in external and observable reality. Spencer's insight, really his paraphrase and generalization of Darwin's, is not quite a truism because it carries the hypothesis that "potential" has an empirical meaning.

Aristotle's idea that potency precedes and explains act is called causality. Adam Smith's friend and fellow Scotsman Hume scarcely doubted causality, but argued correctly (I think) that it cannot be proved either by logic or by experiment. The fittest prove themselves such by surviving if and only if Aristotle was right. Natural selection simply means the probably untestable but little-doubted theory of causality.

Popperians make no sense. Are we supposed to find that a rose is *not* a rose? Or that all reasoning from definition is as transparent as that example? Andrew Wiles' proof of Fermat's last theorem in 1995 ended a search that took

---

[4]   E.g., *Principles of Biology*, 1864.

some pretty bright minds three centuries. My best guess would be that Popperians confuse the concepts of logic and question-begging. They are opposite. Logic (reasoning from assumption and definition) means taking out no more than you put in. Truism or tautology usually means obvious examples of the same, but sometimes includes subtle ones too. Question-begging means taking out what you never put in.[5]

Spencer or Darwin or Gertrude Stein might be faulted for insulting our intelligence by stating the obvious. That shoe would fit Gertrude Stein. But Spencer and Darwin, like the little boy in Hans Christian Andersen's *The Emperor's New Clothes*, were stating the obvious unseen. Andersen's point was that intelligence was not the thing lacking or what the little boy supplied. It was about how tradition and mind-sets and in-groups might sometimes need a look from outside. Peer review is not enough. Sometimes it perpetuates nonsense. The little boy was not a peer, but he could tell clothes when he saw them. ("Peer," as any theorist knows, means someone who pees on your theory.)

I confess that this book casts me as that little boy crashing the economic party, and maybe the evolutionary biology one too, in trust that outsiders might have better chances to spot the obvious unseen. What else was the pay rule? I derived it easily from doctrines already accepted, I think,

---

5   Question-begging claims to take out as inference what it put in as assumption. Assumption that Socrates is a man and that all men are mortal does not confirm that Socrates is a man. It confirms that Socrates is mortal if both assumptions are sound.

and anyhow hard to refute. Those were the total return truism and Ben-Porath's equation for human growth. The maximand rule or deadweight loss rule would prove it as well. How could Becker have missed that what holds for investment in job training by employers holds for any investment by anyone in anything? How could students of the age-wage problem have missed the obvious solution? Investment implies expected recovery with interest, by the investor or a chosen donee, and recovery means recovery of depreciation. I belabor this point because tradition dies hard, and naturally tends to circle wagons under attack. I doubt that my surprise attack will meet the resistance Darwin's found. Darwin's met resistance founded on faith. I took pains to show that my version requires only selection for lineage survival, and that a benign Artificer might ordain the same.

SO WHAT'S NEW?

To claim originality in any field is rash. It is safer to say that some things in this book are new as far as I know. I know at least what I can't remember reading elsewhere. I am more confident in judging what will surprise in the sense of conflict with what is taught today. There we need only keep up with the current conversation. Judging originality with confidence means having read and remembered everything before.

My surprises were not all new, and my novelties (if such) were not all surprises. A few ideas met both descriptions.

The pay rule, and the equally heretical output rule, probably count as both although Becker came within a step of the first. Depreciation theory is also likely to be both. There may also be both surprise and novelty in my suggestion of monetary policy by establishment of real dollars as legal tender.

Free growth theory takes Mill a little farther by ruling out growth by thrift at the collective scale. It should prove a major surprise to lawmakers, who incentivize thrift in the name of growth, and a milder one to economists already prepared by the genius of Solow. My possible originality here was in the growth source equation I derived to test them, the test itself accessing data for market-valued capital as well as consumption from the Piketty-Zucman website, and the free growth hypothesis saying why; the market capitalizes the future. My definitions of market-valued net investment and net output, substituting for the book-valued versions used in national accounts, were essential for testing. I suppose these rank as novelties but not surprises.

The advantage of the growth source equation over the standard lagged output test is great. It avoids the lag, and also gains from the superiority of market measures of capital growth over book ones even when lags end. The method itself is no surprise because the math is high school algebra. The shock is in what it reveals. Solow and Denison were righter than they knew. There is no such thing as capital accumulation at the collective scale.

Risk theory is probably both marginal novelty and marginal surprise. The part that might be new, although obvious in retrospect, is that assets take on the risk characteristics of their owners. We knew all along that people buy assets to fit their own risk profiles. There may be novelty in my idea that it works the same in the opposite direction. Assets once acquired are modified to fit those profiles better. A family home bought by a drug dealer might become a crack house bringing higher expected return at higher risk of confiscation by authorities. Our human capital is untradeable but readily adaptable. Cops can become robbers, and robbers can mend their ways.

Depreciation theory is one of my favorites. It doesn't upset the applecart as much as the pay rule does, because little economic theory depends on it. I love it because it reverses tradition precisely. National accounts model loss of value as starting at a maximum and declining exponentially from an initial minimum. I model it as rising exponentially. It's the same equation with a plus sign in place of a minus sign. I love its obviousness once we think about it. It follows when we remember the present value rule. Once we do, evidence for both factors makes more sense. Depreciation theory rounds out the pay rule in explaining how pay can rise or hold steady to the very end.

And we see the same in business. Gross realized profit, analogous to pay, does not tend to decline as firms approach a date with the wrecking ball. My experience has been that rents go down when properties aren't kept up or locations become unfashionable, but not with age in itself. When it's time to demolish and rebuild, premises I have seen or owned are typically vacated with trade still running at norms. Gross realized output of either factor is inevitably all depreciation on the last day, and would approach zero steadily, rather than hold steady for both factors as we observe, if depreciation did the same.

The physical cash flow rule was probably both new and surprising. Intuition gave no hint that the cash flow of all our belongings together to ourselves equals our consumption less pay plus net gift. There were probably a few heuristic novelties. The parable of the boss and her secretary might itself be new. So might the slave paradox with its parable of Phil and Bill. Many including Adam Smith have pointed out economic inefficiencies in slavery, moral criticism aside. I can't recall mention of this most obvious one. Bill's maintenance consumption was taste-satisfying cash flow to Bill, and capitalized in his present value to himself. It is pure expense to Phil once Bill is enslaved. If all but one of us were enslaved by the one left, national output would drop by all but his own maintenance consumption on the books of the one slave owner.

My critique of Hamilton's rule fixed most of the math problem by allowance for matchers identical in relationship to donees, as parents matching parents, avuncles matching avuncles, grandparents matching grandparents and so forth. The rest of the fix was in reclassifying the new $rmB + A > C$ standard as a target maximand rather than a prerequisite or hurdle rate. I allow banking in my A term generalizing Bob Trivers' reciprocal altruism idea to ease the investment pressure, and to include whatever measure of group selection seems needed. I gave Hamilton's own example where histocompatability genes are preserved at low frequencies until recurrent strains of parasites and pathogens call for them again.

THREE PANTHEONS

A year ago I was being interviewed about my opera *Usher House*. How would I like to be remembered? With a straight face, I said I would like to be thought the best composer since Mahler, the best poet since Masefield, and the best economist since John Stuart Mill. The interviewer looked startled. Was she talking instead to the successor of Don Quixote, Emperor Norton and Walter Mitty?

Probably. But not to worry. Fantasies are good things. They don't become delusions until we start believing them. What I believe is that at least dozens of composers have the knack. There must be hundreds, considering the terrific film scores attributed to names new to me when I hang on for the credits. Each of us, very much including film composers, gives the world what we think it needs. We like to be appreciated, but we don't give a fig what it wants. We won't always agree on what it needs. We'll defend to the death the other guy's right to his message. But we prefer our own. That's what my answer meant. We're each the best. But I do have the temerity to limit the list to those few dozens or hundreds.

Someone might also be surprised at my choice of benchmarks in verse and economics. Masefield and Mill? A consensus might have picked T. S. Elliot, say, and Lord

Keynes. Masefield and Mill are likelier to be remembered as old-fashioned fuddy-duddies already outmoded when they wrote. But that's me. I *am* Don Quixote. Not a single idol in my pantheons in music and verse was born after 1900, and only two in economics.

My pantheon in music holds Bach, Beethoven, Schubert, Wagner and Mahler. Mahler, the last-born, died in 1911 at 51. What about Mozart? Clearly colossal. Listen to the slow movements of almost any of his piano concertos. Childlike simplicity, then a slight surprise, then another, and all at once we are on a trip through the stars. But my top five show us more. Mozart is too darned enigmatic. He is too darned coy. He is too darned third-personal. And I *like* breaking a sweat. Mozart is uniquely the greatest at what he does within the bounds he chooses to set. But I like answers as well as questions. The five in my pantheon give me those.

Mozart is unrivalled at what he does because no one else plays the same game. What other composer has put such a premium on delicacy, on poise, on self-effacement? That doesn't deny that he was a red-blooded *mensch* who loved hijinks and good times as much as the rest of us. His *Rondo alla Turca* is one of many masterpieces showing that side. But it only rounds out the impression of a flawless dinner companion. A maxim of classicism in the Greek spirit is "nothing in excess." Mozart's exuberance and hijinks were just the right amount.

He was the master of moderation. His operas put passion mostly in the mouths of clowns or villains such as Papageno and Osmin and Queen of the Night. His heroes and heroines have feelings too, but keep them circumspect. The perfect companion cares first about our feelings, not his. Mozart remains that even on our journeys together through the stars. We are kept safely away from the heat. We are allowed to feel anxiety because the world is so far below. That was half the point of the trip. The other half is the happy ending as he leads us safely home. Anxiety, but not in excess.

That shows him as the master of levitation. Richard Strauss gives the example of Susanna's aria *"Voi che sapete"* (you who know) from *Figaro,* an innocent ditty which somehow never lands on the tonic (home note) until the end. The beginning of *Eine Kleine Nachtmusik* (a little night music) does this again. But the slow movements of his piano concertos show it best.

Mozart is not in my pantheon, even so. He is moderation in excess. I like the game the others all play. I like a sense of the first person singular. The five in my pantheon also take us through the stars. But they take us closer. We feel the heat because they do. Listen to Bach's *chaconne* for solo violin, or *passacaglia and fugue* for organ. Listen to the *heiliger dankgesang* (holy song of thanksgiving) from Beethoven's quartet opus 132. Listen to the slow movement of Schubert's two-cello quintet opus 163. Listen to Wagner's *liebestod* (love death) from *Tristan,* or Mahler's adagietto from his fifth symphony. This music plays for keeps.

The polar opposite to Mozart would be Verdi. Like Mozart, he is not in my pantheon but close. For Verdi, no passion is too much. He is the master of contrast. He shakes our emotions back and forth as a dog shakes a rat. Lull and storm are each given enough time to pack the most punch in the other. He wants only opposites and extremes. What would the fastidious Franz Joseph have thought? He would have called the guard.

Somewhere between Apollo and Dionysus, between relativism and frenzy, lies the true path. The five in my pantheon have found it.

I seldom call myself a poet, since that's already a tad vainglorious. For better or verse, pun intended, I'm a Jack of that trade too. The true poets in my pantheon begin with Keats and Masefield. I haven't found a clear choice for third. There are awesome things in Milton, Blake, Coleridge, Tennyson, Emily, Houseman, Robinson, Dowson, Yeats and others.

Shakespeare, like Mozart, doesn't figure in the center of the picture. I take him as the greatest mind and soul yet known, the greatest playwright, the greatest writer in general, and all of these because he taps to the bottom of what poetry can be. Hamlet, speaking of Laertes in the gravedigger scene, asks "Who is this whose grief/ Conjures the wandering stars, and makes them stand/ Like wonder-wounded hearers? It is I, /Hamlet the Dane." Holy mackerel! But these are touches in his plays. Poetry, in his time, meant something too coiffed and pretty and mannered for my taste. You can take Venus and Adonis, the Rape of Lucrece, and the sonnets. That includes the petulant dark lady sonnets, which break the model of preciousness but find nothing better. Shakespeare simply came along too early. I credit Milton, in "Lycidas," for discovering the true vein a few decades later.

That leaves economics. Here I really have a one-man pantheon in Sir William Petty. I suppose that I am the only person to have looked at his portrait alongside Isaac Newton's, in the Royal Society which they co-founded, and seen the two as intellectual equals. Mill seems a clear though distant second, thanks to his superb paragraph on growth. The candidates for third seem well behind. Maybe Jevons or John Rae or Leon Walras. Time has not been kind to the teachings of Keynes. I would now rank his teacher Alfred Marshall higher. I like Myrdal's magnificent *ex ante–ex post* distinction. Böhm-Bawerk and the Austrian school are underrated. The pantheon might have room for him.

The two I would squeeze in from the twentieth century are Schultz and Ben-Porath. Schultz' greatest achievement, unless Mincer beat him, was in spotlighting human depreciation and self-invested work. That left me to ask where human depreciation goes. The answer becomes inescapable once we focus on the question. It gives the obvious solution to the age-wage problem. Everything in this book is obvious. Some of it, like that solution, is the obvious but unnoticed.

Somebody, sooner or later, breaks the news about the emperor's new clothes. You'd think Don Quixote would be the last to pipe up. No one in the world was more devoted to tradition and beautiful creatures of the mind. But it takes a fool. He was that, and so am I. *Der reine tor.* There have to be a few of us always. We'll get a few windmills before they get us.

NOTATION

PIKETTY'S r > g ARGUMENT

Piketty, like Solow and most growth economists since publication of the *General Theory*, speaks an economic language which I follow only to a point. I think I could summarize their arguments in their own terms, or those of Harrod of Keynes himself, without quite seeing how conclusions were reached or what they mean at bottom.

Piketty follows Harrod in defining r to mean what I notate $r(K) = P / K$, where P is (net) profit and K is physical capital. He also follows Keynes and Harrod and most modern tradition in defining g as growth rate in output. I notate this $g(Y) = Y / K_T$. My own practice has been to define $r = r(K_T) = Y / K_T$, which is rate of return to total capital rather than to physical capital alone, while defining $g = g(K_T) = \dot{K} / K_T$, the growth rate of total capital rather than of output. I will avoid ambiguity by specifying which is meant as I go along.

I rely on the total return truism $r(K_T) - g(K_T) = c_p$, where c_p is the pure consumption rate C_P / K_T, at the collective scale. Next generation theory predicts $c_p \Rightarrow 1/\text{generation}$ length $\Rightarrow 3.5\%$ per year as an elastic but enduring norm of biology. Data for interest rates and dividend rates seem more or less in this range since Sumerian times (the Homer-Sylla and Global Financial Data reports). Charts and tables, which cannot measure C_p / H_T, seem to confirm at least that C/K is an elastic norm.

My risks theory infers that r(K) should run somewhat lower than $r(K_T)$ because human capital is owned disproportionately by the risk-prone young. Then how might g(Y) compare to $g(K_T)$? The best I have been able to do is to measure Y without the asterisks as $\Delta K + C$ from data for market-valued capital and consumption at the Piketty-Zucman website. I call that sum market-valued output. As for $g(K_T)$, I could do no better than measure g(K) and assume for simplicity that $g(K_T)$ was the same.

My impression from data, and my gut feel, is that industrial economies have shown what I call "elastic balance" for at least the last two centuries. Market-valued capital K, consumption C, and concomitantly market-valued output $\Delta K + C$ have each grown by something over 3% real averaged over cycles. C and K grow almost in lockstep, confirming free growth theory, while $\Delta K + C$ leaps ahead in positive capital accelerations and trails behind in negative ones (decelerations or reversals).

My hunch is that war and recession/depression dislocate and endanger both factors about equally, and so do nothing to change proportions between factor present values H and K, or between factor outputs work W and profit P, or between factor returns $r(H) = W/H$ and $r(K) = P/K$. If so, r(K) holds proportion to $r(K_T)$ throughout, running consistently somewhat lower if I am correct in inferring that human capital is the factor higher in risk and return. g(Y), by these assumptions exceeds $g(K_T)$ in accelerations (good times), lags in decelerations (bad times), and equals it in longer-term average. Then Piketty's $r(K) - g(Y)$ should average something under 3.5% overall, because r(K) figures to fall short of $r(K_T)$, while exceeding whatever that norm is in good times and lagging it in bad times.

Piketty's view agrees in some respects. He models $r(K)-g(Y)$ as 3.5% to 4.5% in the preindustrial period, for reasons unclear to me, and less during the industrial revolution. He sees it as shrinking again in the period of world wars, world depression and welfare state from 1914 through 1970 or so, and then rising again with restoration of free markets. He sees the new norm for $r(K)-g(Y)$ as about 3%, which sounds about right to me, but infers as I do not that this much margin risks an increase in Harrod's capital share P/Y.

I have some idea why he thinks so. He accepts a popular doctrine, dating from Harrod's time, that profit tends to be invested while pay tends to be consumed. Many today follow this plausible belief to an inference that tax cuts for us rich are good for growth and employment. Piketty sees the same outcome, if I understand him, and stresses the widening of inequality while they stress those benefits.

The charts and tables, drawn ironically from the Piketty-Zucman website, suggest that the popular doctrine is wrong. Cutback is futility. Less invested consumption means so much less human capital by definition, while less pure consumption expected means less present value of total capital unless the saving is invested more productively. The principle of diminishing returns predicts that it will not be. Neither pay nor profit will in fact be invested beyond depreciation plowback because investors somehow know this at bottom. Their expectations, subliminal if not rational, smell diminishing returns around the corner. Something in us knows that the first priority is to maintain the value of capital in place, meaning obviously our own human capital but subtly all physical capital too, by fulfilling the expected consumption on which both depend.

Piketty's great contribution is in his scholarship and website. We seem to be alike in our enthusiasm for economic history and insights of the past. The golden age he invokes is the "years of high theory" running roughly from Cobb and Douglas in the 1920s through Keynes and Harrod in the thirties and forties to Solow in the fifties. I personally think that his magnificent research has obsoleted them all. If they had begun with information on market-valued capital, collated and extended at his website, the difference in what and how they reasoned might have been profound. Why would have Harrod have modeled the capital/output ratio in dividing saving rate $s = \Delta K / Y$ by $g_Y = \Delta Y / Y$ to find $\Delta K / \Delta Y$, which equals K/Y only if K/Y is constant, when he might have measured K and $\Delta K + C$ directly as the Piketty-Zucman website allows me to do? That website is Exhibit A in my case for starting macro over from scratch. Macro never had a chance before. Now it has one.

HOW TO SOLVE TESTS

The next time you are in a nightmare where you must answer questions in economics of which you cannot understand a word, except the occasional conjunction or preposition, write down "maximization of risk-adjusted rate of return." You will get a F anyhow, since it's a nightmare, but at least you will have the satisfaction of knowing the answer was right. r in my Y/K_T sense is the elephant in every room in economics, for one metaphor, or the light switch for another. It is what both Piketty and the Freedom Caucus miss in supposing that more profit portends more investment or higher capital shares. Both sides miss the maximand rule. More money to spend does not mean more spending, as Lucas knew, unless it adds value by lifting return to cost over return to market.

The charts and tables don't tell us whether or not growth through cutback has even been attempted at the collective scale. They say only that any such attempt will have failed. My hunch is that substantially none has been attempted unless by government. The convergence axioms give us credit for smelling bad deals around the corner. Government has special concerns that might mask the smell or misplace the light switch. That's one reason why I'm a huge free market fan. Ironically, economists might be likelier to miss them than ordinary duffers like the undersigned. Smelling lies outside logical analysis.

Piketty and the Freedom Caucus, from their outside specialties in economics and government, miss what we unenlightened folk somehow sense. We will not invest either pay or gross profit in anything beyond depreciation plowback, collectively, because a subliminal hand puts that money back in our pockets. Within that limit, we do not earmark investments from gross profit into K alone, or from pay into H alone, but allocate to maximize their sum. Meanwhile the subliminal hand of biology allocates just enough gift to just the right donees to keep the generations turning.

One of the most poignant ironies of science and philosophy is that we leave subliminal wisdom in Plato's cave, and in the custody of poets, until reason reconstructs it at last. That's how my unaccountable hunch, given Piketty's indispensable data base, evolved into free growth theory. Hunch, evidence, and finally the rationale. I suspect that the part of all of us that never left Plato's cave knew it all along.

Not that I advocate moving back. I like the view from here. Ancestral Eve, or her descendants about 50,000 years ago, committed us to a path in the dark. We find the light by stages, and try our luck in the darkness beyond. We always have carfare back to the cave when music and poetry are the call, or the unaccountable hunches that precede evidence and rationale. That's what I like.

The view for macro is what I like most. Its golden age starts now. Keynes and Harrod and Solow belong to its heroic age which cleared the wilderness to build logical structures before Piketty assembled the means to obsolete them. A supreme irony is that Piketty himself, as a theorist rather than researcher, has chosen the heroic age by accepting net national product as output, and leaving duffers like the undersigned to reinterpret ΔK as change in market-valued capital shown at his website, not as book net investment, and to reinterpret $\Delta K + C$ the same way.

It seems to me that the true years of high theory continued into the 1960s, and peaked in them. The contributions that will last into the golden age seem to come most from Schultz and Ben-Porath. That's why they fit into my pantheon. They developed the insights of pure and invested consumption, of human depreciation and of self-invested work that nearly complete the picture of human capital drawn from Petty through Farr and Walras and Fisher. What seems to have been left to this duffer is explicit analysis of where human depreciation goes. A reasonably clear innuendo in the Ben-Porath model, and I think in Schultz and most tradition, Becker perhaps aside, is that it goes six feet under in deadweight loss.

One can appreciate the indelicacy of saying so outright. This duffer, inured to indelicacy in lawsuits and boardroom battles, would not have shrunk from that. But hunch, and then logical certainty in this case, produced the possibly even more indelicate recovery rule. The pay rule relied further on the maintenance exhaust assumption, which is probably unprovable but bolstered by the parable of the boss and her secretary.

The golden age of macro, and the new years of high theory, had better make peace with indelicacy. Spades are spades. This book, while exogenizing growth at least as far as Solow, proposes to endogenize human capital as a kind of final link in the value-added chain. Talk about indelicacy! Many still find euphemisms for human capital itself, as Fisher did in his great books of 1906 and 1907.

Certainly we don't want gratuitous indelicacy, which is childish potty language. I took pains to keep that out. Human capital, I said, is not our souls or even our bodies, and it is not for sale. It is present value of our skill sets to ourselves as the only possible owner. I fear that's about as much delicacy as I can manage while calling a spade a spade. Economics is not famous for tact in any case. The dismal science can be confirmed as the blunt one.

Plato's Socrates told us to follow the argument wherever it leads. It led him to the hemlock, me to the heresies herein. Where I have botched the job, others can do it right. Ducking the question is what I do not expect of golden ages and high theory. Praise the Lord, pass the hemlock, and send us more indelicate questions. The answer is maximization of risk-adjusted rate of return.

GLOSSARY

I use standard terms when I can find them, or adapt them as in changing Schultz's "pure investment" to "invested consumption," and coin new ones like "cutback" and "net gift" when I can't. But even standard ones are ambiguous. The vocabulary of economics is not settled. Look up "capital" or "output" or "cash flow," for example, in any economic dictionary. It will show ranges of meanings, and appreciably different ones from one dictionary to the next. I coped by defining as I went along, and would have had to do the same even if this book were meant for economists only. Otherwise the ambiguities would have left loopholes. My definitions include:

acceleration: change in capital growth.
anti-Keynesian: opposing fiscal and monetary policy in the Keynesian senses.
bioeconomics: economic specialty applying biological principles.

biological imperative: traits are selected to prioritize survival and reproduction.

capital: means of aims; human plus physical capital; present value of expected cash flows.

cash flow: capital passed out, in transfer or exhaust, less capital inserted from outside.

constant dollars: dollar value as of a specified year.

crowding in: enhancement of prospective return by government investment.

crowding out: lowering prospective return by preemptive government investment.

current cost accounting: accounting which adjusts book assets upward for inflation since date booked.

cutback: change in consumption/capital ratio or pure consumption/total capital ratio times minus one. Negative when that change is positive.

deadweight loss: decapitalization not recovered in transfer or pure consumption.

depreciation: recovery of at-cost investment in revenue and gross realized output.

depreciation theory: depreciation of both factors rises gradually from negligibility at the start to substantially all of gross realized output at the end.

derivative: security which adjusts value to performance of another security.

discounted cash flow: valuation of capital as the sum (integral) of expected cash flows discounted by the time preference rate. Same as present value.

economics: any quantitative rationale of choices.

equity: ownership net of debt and other outside claims.

exchange-traded fund (ETF): mutual fund trading depository receipts instantaneously rather than daily.

exhaust: termination of capital in taste satisfaction.

exogenous: sourced from outside, meaning outside the current model or discussion.

fiscal policy: tax cuts and more government spending in slumps, and the reverse in booms.

flow: any process measured in capital per unit time.

free growth index: productivity gain/capital acceleration rate.

free growth theory: prediction that the free growth index will converge to unity at very large scales.

free growth: investment at market less investment at cost.

gene frequency: percentage representation of all copies of an allele vis-à-vis all its competitors at the same gene site throughout the population.

generation length: average age difference between parents and offspring. I follow R. A. Fisher's method equal-weighting both parents and all births from first to last.

gift received: transfer in from capital of another individual.

gift: transfer out to capital of another individual.

gross realized work: realized work plus recovered human depreciation.

Hamilton's rule: creatures are selected to invest in conspecifics so as to maximize rb – c, where c is fitness surrendered by the donor, benefit b is fitness gained by the donee, and r is relatedness between.

heuristics: philosophy or rationale of teaching.

histocompatibility genes: genes regulating parasite and
pathogen resistance.

human capital: present value of skill sets; capital whose
outside operating cost is exhausted in taste satisfaction;
present value of pay less invested consumption; present
cost of past invested consumption less pay.

human cash flow: pay less invested consumption.

human depreciation: elapse of human capital as time dimin-
ishes the stream of remaining future pay to be discounted to present value.

income: rights to output; equal to output.

invested consumption: all good and services, other than
self-invested work, which are converted into human
capital. Includes schooling.

investment: in my word equations, investment means actual
growth of physical capital.

Keynesian: favoring fiscal and monetary policy in the
Keynesian senses.

lagged output method: evaluation of investment effectiveness by observing change in output after a lapse in time.

last day paradox: inference from the present value equation
that human capital equals a little less than one day's pay
at the start of the last day, then one hour's at the start
of the last hour and so forth. If pay measured realized
output of human capital, productivity or return to human
capital would begin the last day at more than 100%
per day, and would rise to infinity at the last moment.
Yet risk theory reasons that time discount rate of all
assets including human capital is revealed as that of our

security portfolios, where it runs only a few percent per year and declines rather than rises with age.

macro: same as macroeconomics.

macroeconomics: policies to reconcile full employment of plant and workers with stable money value at national scales.

maintenance exhaust principle: argument from the biological imperative that maintenance consumption is exhausted in satisfying our taste for individual and lineage survival.

maintenance learning: learning necessary to realize current pay as distinct from learning to augment future pay.

maintenance schooling: adult schooling to update current skills and maintain current pay rather than add skills for higher later pay.

market-valued investment: change in market-valued capital rather than book net investment.

market-valued output: consumption plus market-valued investment.

micro: same as microeconomics.

microeconomics: study of the interplay of supply, demand and price at all scales.

monetary policy (Austrian school or Friedman): stable money supply, growing at the projected long-term real growth rate of the economy, whether in boom or bust.

monetary policy (Keynesian): interest rate reduction and money supply increase in slumps, and the reverse in booms.

net gift: gift less gift received.

net transfer: transfer out less transfer in.

next generation theory: average-risk cash flow rate converges to the reciprocal of the generation length.

omnibus fund: balanced index fund designed to prioritize liquidity while representing the whole economy
in microcosm.

output: creation of wealth, or equivalently of capital of
either factor.

output rule: inference from the total return truism and
Ben-Porath equation that output equals investment
plus consumption plus self-invested work less human
depreciation.

owner rule: we choose or adapt capital of both factors to
fit our current risk tolerance.

pay rule: inference from the recovery rule and maintenance
exhaust principle that human depreciation is expected
to be recovered in pay while maintenance consumption
is exhausted.

pay: revenue of human capital. Same as wage.

period of production theory: rate of return means rate of
production, and therefore equals the reciprocal of the
period of production. Taught by Rae, Senior, Jevons,
Böhm-Bawerk and much of the Austrian school. True by
definition, but uninformative unless we reason in terms
of total capital as in next generation theory.

physical capital: capital whose outside operating cost does
not satisfy tastes.

physiocrats: eighteenth-century economists led by Francios
Quesnay who taught that maintenance consumption is

recovered in product value and that only land should be taxed.

present cost: valuation of capital as the sum (integral) of past cash flows times minus one compounded by the time preference rate.

productivity gain: change in productivity.

productivity: output/physical capital or output/total capital.

profit: output of physical capital.

proprietary output: output of either factor not yet sold or not meant to be sold. Self-invested work in the case of human capital.

pure consumption: same as exhaust.

rate: quantity measured as a flow over a stock, and equivalently as a pure number over time.

realized work: work marketed for pay rather than self-invested.

reciprocal: multiplicative inverse; one over a quantity.

replacement cost accounting: current cost accounting with a further change to replace linear depreciation with a curve believed more realistic.

risk theory: we trade or adjust assets of both factors (human and physical capital) to fit current risk tolerance.

round trip truism: r in the market return and time preference senses must always agree.

self-invested work: work invested in the worker's own human capital. Work invested in someone else's is included within the recipient's invested consumption.

slave paradox: to enslave someone is to subtract his maintenance consumption from his output and from the economy's, and to subtract its present value from his human capital. Thus a restoration of slave markets would reveal less than the value of human capital to ourselves.

social return: net benefit to all including non-transactors.

stock: quantity measured in dollars alone. Same as capital.

tastes: intentions whose satisfaction terminates capital in exhaust.

three-fourths rule: estimate that human capital and pure consumption are three-fourths of total capital and total consumption respectively.

thrift index: cutback/capital acceleration rate.

time preference: time discount rate.

total return truism: output equals capital growth plus cash flow.

transfer in: value inserted from outside, net of payment or reciprocation. Same as new investment from outside.

transfer out: value passed out and recovered fully in other assets rather than exhausted, net of payment or reciprocation.

unity: the number one.

W doctrine: teaching that work equals wage (pay).

wage: same as pay.

work: output of human capital.

Y doctrine or *Y = I + C doctrine*: teaching that output equals investment plus consumption.